Following God

LEARNING LIFE PRINCIPLES FROM THE PERSONALITIES OF THE OLD TESTAMENT

LEARNING LIFE PRINCIPLES FROM THE PERSONALITIES OF THE OLD TESTAMENT

A Bible Study by

Wayne Barber
Eddie Rasnake
Richard Shepherd

 AMG Publishers™

Chattanooga, TN 37422

Following God

LEARNING LIFE PRINCIPLES FROM THE PERSONALITIES OF THE OLD TESTAMENT

© 1998 by Wayne A. Barber, Eddie Rasnake, and Richard L. Shepherd

Revised Edition 1999
Fifth Printing 2002

Published by AMG Publishers

ISBN: 0-89957-300-2

Printed in the United States of America.
07 06 05 04 03 02 -E- 10 9 8 7 6 5

This book is dedicated to
Spiros Zodhiates
mentor, model, and friend.

Acknowledgements

This work goes forth with a special thank you to our wives, Diana, Michele and Linda Gail, who have shown us much about following God. Special thanks also go to Jennifer Ould and Troy Renfrow who took something good and made it great. Thanks to all the folks at AMG, especially Trevor Overcash, Tasos Ioannidis, Dale Anderson and Vince Stone (cover design) for believing in this project. Thanks to Jenny Smith for polishing the product, and Phillip Rodgers for his artistic direction and dedication. And thanks to the test group who showed us where we needed work. Most of all we are grateful to the Lord Jesus, who continues to teach and train each of us in what it means to follow Him with a whole heart.

 THE AUTHORS

Wayne Barber

WAYNE BARBER has recently become Senior Pastor of Hoffmantown Church, Albuquerque, NewMexico. A renowned national and international conference ministry speaker, the primary goal of Wayne's ministry is in spreading the message of "the sufficiency of Christ." People around the world connect with Wayne's unique ability to make God's Word come alive through his honest and open "real-life" experiences. Wayne has authored or co-authored several books, and his most recent book, *The Rest of Grace*, was published in 1998. He also authors a regular column in AMG's *Pulpit Helps* monthly magazine. For eighteen years he served as Senior Pastor-Teacher of Woodland Park Baptist Church, in Chattanooga, Tennessee, and for many of those years in Chattanooga, Wayne co-taught with noted author Kay Arthur of Precept Ministries and has studied under Dr. Spiros Zodhiates, one of the world's leading Greek scholars. Wayne and his wife Diana have two grown children and will soon make their home in Albuquerque.

Rick Shepherd

RICHARD L. SHEPHERD has served as an associate pastor focusing on areas of teaching, discipleship, and prayer for more than twenty years. He has served in churches in Alabama, Florida, and Texas, and has ministered at Woodland Park Baptist Church in Chattanooga, Tennessee since 1983. The Lord's ministry has taken him to several countries, including Haiti, Romania, Ukraine, Moldova, Italy, England, Greece, and Israel. Some of the specific ministries Rick has been involved in include training pastors, church leaders, and congregations, with further involvement as a teacher on college and seminary campuses. Rick graduated with honors from the University of Mobile and holds a Master of Divinity and a Ph.D. from Southwestern Theological Seminary in Fort Worth, Texas. He and his wife Linda Gail have four children and make their home in Chattanooga, Tennessee.

Eddie Rasnake

EDDIE RASNAKE met Christ in 1976 as a freshman in college. He graduated with honors from East Tennessee State University in 1980. He and his wife, Michele, served for nearly seven years on the staff of Campus Crusade for Christ. Their first assignment was the University of Virginia, and while there they also started a Campus Crusade ministry at James Madison University. Eddie then served four years as campus director of the Campus Crusade ministry at the University of Tennessee. In 1989, Eddie left Campus Crusade to join Wayne Barber at Woodland Park Baptist Church as the Associate Pastor of Discipleship and Training. He has been ministering in Eastern Europe in the role of equipping local believers for more than a decade and has published materials in Albanian, German, Greek, Italian, Romanian, and Russian. Eddie serves on the boards of directors of the Center for Christian Leadership in Tirana, Albania, and the Bible Training Center in Eleuthera, Bahamas. He also serves as chaplain for the Chattanooga Lookouts (Cincinnati Reds AA affiliate) baseball team. Eddie and his wife Michele live in Chattanooga, Tennessee, with their four children.

THE SERIES:

Three authors and fellow ministers, Wayne Barber, Eddie Rasnake, and Rick Shepherd, teamed up in 1998 to write a character-based Bible study for AMG Publishers. Their collaboration developed into the title, *Life Principles from the Old Testament*. Since 1998 these same authors and AMG Publishers have produced five more character-based studies—each consisting of twelve lessons geared around a five-day study of a particular Bible personality. More studies of this type are in the works. Two new titles were added to the series in 2001: *Life Principles for Worship from the Tabernacle* and *Living God's Will*. These newest titles are unique in that they are the first Following God™ studies that are topically-based rather than Bible character-based. However, the interactive study format that readers have come to love remains constant with each new release. As new titles are being planned, our focus remains the same: to provide excellent Bible study materials that point people to God's Word in ways that allow them to apply truths to their own lives. More information on this groundbreaking series can be found on the following web pages:

www.followingGod.com
www.amgpublishers.com

Preface

Noah and the ark...Jacob's ladder of angels...Joseph's coat of many colors...Moses and the burning bush...Joshua and the Battle of Jericho...Samson and Delilah.

All of these are stories many of us have been familiar with since we were children, and they're the same stories we tell our own children. But they're so much more than just entertaining stories or history. It can be all too easy to see these people as merely characters. In fact, that's what we often call them—"Bible characters." But they are so much more than that!

They're real people, with all the joys and sorrows, successes and failures, satisfaction and disappointment that make up life. They're people who had to learn to follow God through all kinds of circumstances, and even stumbled on occasion. And God recorded their lives for a purpose: so we can learn from them what God is like and what it means to follow Him.

Each of the men in this study found that out in their own unique way, and as you look at their lives you'll soon realize that there's no formula to following God. There are only principles He's given us, and examples to look at, listen to, and learn from.

Following God is a journey, and the path is not always easy, but we can be assured of His presence with us. Sometimes the trail isn't marked as clearly as we'd like, but that's where we find the riches of the wisdom of our Guide and Friend, the Lord Jesus. He knows which way to go. He walked with each of these men, and He walks with each of us today. All we need to do is surrender and follow.

And that's what we'd like to invite you to do with us. Come along on this twelve-week journey of following God with Noah, Abraham, Moses, and so many more. You'll learn much about these men, and you'll find they may not be all that different from you. But most of all, you'll see the Lord in new ways. It is our prayer that this will lead to the joy and rest of a deeper surrender to Him and His ways and a lifetime of following God.

WAYNE A. BARBER   RICHARD L. SHEPHERD

EDDIE RASNAKE

Table of Contents

FOLLOWING GOD'S DESIGN

Genesis means "beginnings"—it is God's Book of Beginnings: the beginning of creation, the beginnings of Adam and Eve, of marriage and family, of life on this earth. In it, we find answers to some of the basic questions of life such as: Who is God and what is He like? Who is man, and why was he created? Is what we see now the way God meant for life to be? What do we do to fix the problems we see now? In addition, each of us has personal questions like what is God's purpose for me and how do I fit into God's design? These and other questions begin to be answered when we look into the record of Genesis, for Genesis is not simply the record of Adam's beginnings, it is also the record of our beginnings. It helps us understand our journey through time into eternity—our journey in learning and walking in the ways of God, knowing what it means to follow God and experience the joy and adventure of that daily walk with Him.

How do I fit into God's design?

WHERE DOES HE FIT?

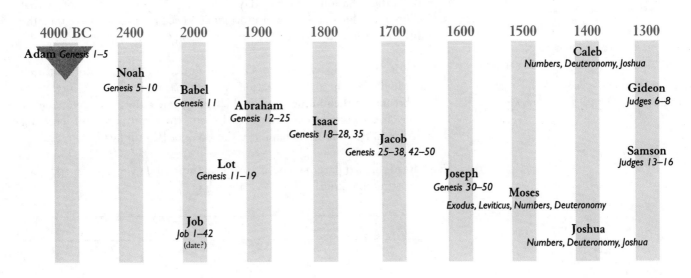

GOD'S DESIGN FOR MAN

What do we learn from Adam about God's design for man? If we were to sit down with Adam and look at his family photo album, what pictures would he point out as significant? What things would we read from the first days of his diary or journal? When we turn to the first pages of Scripture we find the things God says are significant and the things He wants us to know and apply concerning His design for us.

First, let's take a quick overview of creation. Genesis chapter one, verses 1–23, describes the first five days of creation. In these verses, God creates light (day 1), He makes the sky (day 2), He provides dry land with plants and trees (day 3), He creates the sun, moon, and stars (day 4), He fills the waters and the sky with fish and birds (day 5), and in day 6, He makes *"the beasts of the earth after their kind."* All creatures, so far, were made alive by the simple declaration of God—He spoke the animals, birds, and fish into existence (Genesis 1:20–24). His next and final creation would be different. Up to this point, God had not created anything that could personally relate to Him. Later on the sixth day, God created man.

📖 Read Genesis 2:7, 16–17. List at least three ways God's creation of man was different from His other creations.

_____

_____

_____

_____

Word Study
THE WORDS OF CREATION

Yatsar ("form")—to initiate and structure or construct something (as would a skilled potter in clay or a carver in wood)

'Aphar ("dust")—dry earth, fine dust, or clay from the surface of the ground

'Adhamah ("ground")—source of the name "Adam," meaning "reddish earth"

Da'ath ("knowledge")—from *yadha* meaning "experiential active knowing"

First, man was created or formed (*yatsar*) by God Himself out of the fine dust of the ground. God worked as a skilled artist to make this unique creation. Second, God then uniquely breathed into man the breath of life. In Proverbs 20:27 the word for *"breath"* refers to the spirit of man, with the idea of man's conscience or capacity for moral reasoning. When God breathed into the face of Adam, He not only put that life breath in his nostrils, He also gave Adam something of His person or personality. Adam became a living soul with a likeness to God—here was man in the image of God! Man was a God-breathed creation uniquely related to the Creator and designed to walk in that relationship every day—all day. The third distinction is that God imparted life marked by immortality (v. 17). Fourth, God gave man the ability to reason and choose his course of action (v. 17).

From the beginning, we see that God had something more in store for man than He did for the rest of creation. We see that man was able to relate to God because of the unique way in which He created him. What were God's reasons for creating man? God spells out three purposes for creating mankind in the very first chapter of the Book of Beginnings.

📖 Read the first part of Genesis 1:26. What was God's very first purpose for creating mankind?

_____

_____

God wants us to bear His image. This does not mean that we are exactly like God—rather, it means that we reflect what He is like. We are like the reflection in a mirror. When you look in the mirror in the morning, what you see is not another you, but a reflection of you. Once you leave, that reflection is gone. It has no real life apart from you.

Why do you think God would have made man in His own image?

_____

_____

_____

Man was designed to reflect the image of God so that a personal relationship between God and man would be possible. Man was designed to walk with God in a unique person-to-person, heart-to-heart, mind-to-mind, spirit-to-spirit relationship. He is made for oneness with His Creator and Lord. Out of that oneness we can begin to see life for what it was meant to be: a relationship first with God, then with others. Walking in that oneness is the only way to follow God and know and do His will. That is God's design. For God's life to be reflected in us, we must walk with Him day by day.

📖 Read the first part of Genesis 1:28. What do you see as a second purpose for mankind?

_____

_____

Man was designed to walk with God in a unique person-to-person, heart-to-heart, mind-to-mind, spirit-to-spirit relationship.

Not only does God want us to reflect Him, but He wants us to reproduce that reflection—to have and to raise children who will also reflect Him. Fruit is the expression of the nature and life of a person or thing. The bearing of children means more than giving birth to little humans. It means raising them to become mature image-bearers who clearly display, express, and explain the image of God wherever they go throughout the earth. This requires not just procreation, but also parenting—raising children in the nurture and admonition of the Lord so that they reflect Him instead of the sinful propensities of man apart from God.

Once you understand how large the earth is, you realize that Adam and Eve alone could not reign over all of it by themselves. This explains why the Lord instructs Adam and Eve first to be fruitful and multiply so they can fill the earth, and then subdue it.

📖 From the remainder of verses 26 and 28, summarize into one sentence a third purpose God had for mankind.

_____

_____

As the image of God is reflected in us and then reproduced through us, we can reign over His creation in a way that reflects what He is like.

Since God's purpose for mankind includes reigning over creation, what purpose does the rest of creation serve (vv. 28–31)?

_____

_____

_____

The plants and trees are to serve mankind and the animals by providing food. In Genesis 9:3 we see animals added to man's sources of food. All of the created realm is to serve mankind. That is wrapped up in the idea of the word *"subdue"* in verse 28. All of creation is to be tamed, to be brought into submission. It is right and fitting in the plan of God for a horse to provide mankind with transportation, a cow with milk, an oxen or donkey with manual strength for tilling the earth. The term subdue communicates not only that creation is to serve mankind, but that mankind is to be a steward of creation. Today our world has gone to two extremes that miss the mark of God's design. One facet of society has ceased to be a good steward of the creation over which God placed mankind as caretakers. Pollution, waste, and mismanagement of our natural resources—these are evidences of failing to be a good steward of creation. Another facet of our society has reacted to these mistakes and pushed the pendulum to the opposite extreme. This group has abdicated our role as the centerpiece of creation and has ceased to allow creation to serve mankind as it was designed. Those who argue against fur coats should be reminded that God made the first fur coats. Genesis 3:21 states that *". . . the LORD God made garments of skin for Adam and his wife, and clothed them."*

📖 Read Genesis 2:7–9 and 3:8. What specific purposes did God have for creating the garden over which man was to reign?

_____

_____

_____

Put Yourself In Their Shoes

"THE GARDEN OF DELIGHT"

Eden means "delight" and was meant to be a place where God and man would walk in the delight of a loving relationship. Are you experiencing delight in your personal relationship with the Lord?

The garden of Eden was a planned environment. One of the things we see here is that the plants of the garden were created not only for food, but also for beauty. Imagine what it must have been like to stroll through that garden and witness every tree and plant that is "*. . . pleasing to the sight.*" In fact, the name *"Eden"* means "delight." None of the animals were able to appreciate that beauty like mankind could. The garden of Eden was uniquely created for mankind. But it was also a place for God. Genesis 3:8, though it occurs in the context of the fall of mankind, speaks loudly of fellowship with God. Not only was the garden a place for mankind to walk, but the Lord used to walk there in the cool of the day. Before sin, mankind walked in fellowship with the Creator.

From what we have seen so far about why God created man and the instructions He gave him, we can summarize the purpose of man in three foundational statements:

1. Mankind is to reflect (or express) the image of God—God's very life, which includes His character and His care for life around Him.

2. Mankind is to reproduce that image (to bear fruit) through children raised to reflect the image of God.

3. Mankind is to reign in life in a way that reflects God. In Scripture the idea of reigning is serving by leading. It means maintaining self-control so that we can give ourselves to serving and caring for others and for the creation.

Man was created in the image of God to reign over the earth. He was to bear the fruit of children who would carry the image and likeness of God throughout the earth. As a result, their reign would be further expanded. But what were they to do within this design God had given? What were God's directions for man? Genesis 2 gives us further insight.

📖 Read Genesis 2:15–17. What three directions did God give to the man?

_____

_____

_____

Man was to first of all "*cultivate*" or grow the Garden, experiencing God's provision and satisfaction. This would help insure that creation served him to its fullest potential. Second, he was to "*keep*" or guard the garden, thus walking in protection and security. This would help insure that he was the best steward of creation that he could be. And third, he was directed not to eat from "*the tree of the knowledge of good and evil*," which required him to walk in obedience, experiencing the goodness of God—the "very good" of all that surrounded him. This was God's call for him to live submitted. God created mankind to have freedom within boundaries. As long as he lived in submission to God and as a faithful steward of creation, he would be served by creation in ways that are both sustaining and satisfying. But if he stepped outside the boundaries or if he neglected his responsibilities, he would fail. That obedience included consciously avoiding the tree of the knowledge of good and evil, and thus walking in a chosen moral goodness and purity in all of life.

The full meaning of the purposes of God is carried out in daily life as we grow and guard what has been given to us in the place God has put us (just as Adam was supposed to do). There we experience His good, acceptable, and perfect will (Romans 12:2), as we walk in the good works He has prepared for us to do (Ephesians 2:10).

God created man to reflect His image, to reproduce that image in his children, and to reign over creation in a way consistent with that image. But in each of these assignments, relationship is paramount. Adam could fulfill none of this design on his own. He was dependent on God to see these things become a reality in his life.

📜 **Word Study**
CULTIVATE AND KEEP

Abad ("cultivate")—meaning "to nourish, nurture," to cause to grow to maturity, to reach full life and fruitfulness.

Shamar ("keep")—meaning "to guard," to protect from harm or danger or from any threat to life and fruitfulness.

> *Adam could fulfill none of this design on his own. He was dependent on God to see these things become a reality in his life.*

Adam  DAY TWO

"ADAM, WHERE ARE YOU?"

One of the marks of the "very good" creation was the peace or harmony evident in the Garden and in the created order. The idea of "good" throughout Scripture carries with it the idea of peace. In relationships it is seen in two coming together in oneness and harmony, with no division, no strife or fighting.

We saw in Day One that God created Adam with a design in view. He placed mankind in the center of His work with a clearly defined purpose. But it is important to realize that Adam could not fulfill God's purpose for his life apart from God. God's intent for mankind first and foremost is that we glorify Him by reflecting His image on planet earth. Everything else flows out of that preeminent purpose.

In Day One we used the analogy of a mirror. Let me suggest another analogy. Consider the moon—it lights up the night sky. When the moon is full it gives enough light so that one can travel freely at night with no other source of illumination. But the moon has no real light of its own, it merely reflects the light of the sun. If the sun stopped shining, the moon would be black. In fact, unless the moon is facing the sun, it has no light at all to give to us. When something stands between the moon and the sun it ceases to give light. We call this an eclipse. The moon cannot fulfill its purpose apart from the sun.

In the same way, man derives his purpose from God and is dependent on God to fulfill His purpose. If man ceases to walk in relationship with God, he ceases to reflect the life of God. The image of God is eclipsed—it can no longer be seen. Not only that, but if man is not facing God, walking in fellowship with Him, and reflecting Him, then it is impossible for man to reproduce what God desires. Without the light of God, his darkness bears children of darkness. Without oneness with the Creator it is also impossible for man to reign in life in a way that reflects God. We want to look at interrupted oneness and its disastrous effect on God's desires being fulfilled.

📖 Read Genesis 3:1–6. What do you see from verses 4 and 5 that the serpent offered Eve?

_____

_____

_____

In Genesis 2:16–17 we saw that in order for man to subdue the earth as he should, he had to live submitted to the boundaries God had set for him—he had to walk in oneness with the will of God. Yet Satan called both the truthfulness and the goodness of God's will into question. He tempted Adam and Eve first of all to doubt the truthfulness of what God had said (*"You surely shall not die"*), and then to doubt the goodness of God's motives. Satan enticed them to believe that God was withholding something of value from them.

In verse 6, what did Eve do in response?

_____

_____

What did Adam do (v. 6)?

_____

_____

The serpent came tempting Eve to eat of the forbidden tree which she knew was off limits. She was deceived and ate. She then gave the fruit to Adam who chose to eat.

According to Genesis 3:7 what were the immediate results of their choice?

    a. They sewed fig leaves together to cover themselves.

    b. They knew they were naked.

    c. Their innocence was gone.

    d. All of the above.

Man derives his purpose from God and is dependent on God to fulfill His purpose.

Extra Mile

THE DAMAGE OF SIN

Read Genesis chapters 4—6 reflectively looking at the damage sin did to the image of God being reflected by mankind.

Make a list of the attitudes and actions you observe in these chapters, and identify:

• What do they reflect?

• What is being reproduced?

• What characterized man's reign?

How did their choice cause them to respond to their Creator (vv. 8–13)?

_____

_____

_____

The disastrous outcome of their choice not to follow God was a total eclipse of oneness. Instead of walking with God, they hid from Him. Instead of joy, the relationship now held fear. They had allowed something to come between them and the light, and now they stood in darkness.

In verses 12–13, how did Adam and Eve's choices affect their oneness with each other and with God?

_____

_____

_____

As a result of their sin, Adam and Eve recognized their wrong. With their sin came guilt, fear, shame, and an attempt to cover up. God came asking Adam, *"where are you?"* Knowing Adam had sinned, God wanted him to admit it. Instead, Adam and Eve played the "blame game." Adam's response is telling. In one sentence he tries to blame both Eve (*". . . the woman"*) and God (*". . . whom Thou gavest me"*) for his sinful choice. Eve too, joined in this game of blame (*"The serpent deceived me. . ."*). Sin had shattered the oneness with God that they had experienced. Instead of a oneness with God there was division and running away from God. Instead of honesty between themselves and their Creator, there were blame and excuses. The oneness between Adam and Eve was gone as well. In its place were separation, blame, and disharmony. With Adam's disobedience, sin entered the human race. Instead of life and oneness with God, they experienced death and separation.

Adam and Eve's choice to follow their own will instead of following God affected not only them, but the design of God as well. The image of God could no longer be clearly seen in mankind. Remember the mirror of which we spoke—that we are to reflect God like a mirror reflects our face? Now the mirror is muddied; it is stained by sin. One could still see glimpses of the former glory, but God could no longer be clearly seen in mankind. It was as if the mirror was now shattered into pieces.

Not only did sin negate mankind's ability to reflect the image of God, but it also stained what man reproduced.

Read Genesis 4:1–8. What impact did sin have on the offspring of Adam and Eve?

_____

_____

_____

Welcome to the first dysfunctional family! Though Adam and Eve were created in the image of God, rebellion crept in, and thus the struggle between good and evil intensified. The children Adam and Eve bore gave evidence of this same struggle between good and evil. One son (Abel) followed God, and the other (Cain) did not.

Doctrine
COVER-UP

Adam's and Eve's "fig-leaf fashions" could not cover their guilt, shame, and fear. It was the best they could do, and it was useless. Only God can cover our sins. Physically, God gave Adam and Eve garments of skin (lasting leather). These garments suggest that an animal was sacrificed and symbolically spoke of atonement—the covering of sin by the blood of God's chosen sacrifice. Jesus is that sacrifice for us, the Lamb of God, who not only covers our sin but takes away our sin (John 1:29).

📖 Read Genesis 5:3. Whose image did the children of Adam bear?

_____

_____

_____

Instead of reflecting the image of God, the children bore the image of fallen Adam. He *". . . became the father of a son in his **own** likeness, according to **his** image. . ."*(emphasis added).

📖 Read Genesis 6:5. What did the image of man now reflect?

_____

_____

_____

When Adam turned from God and ceased to reflect His image, the whole design of God was compromised. Now, the image of man, instead of reflecting God took on a brutal new look. It reflected wicked actions, evil thoughts, and evil intent. And of course, this had a cataclysmic effect on humans being able to reign over creation in a way that would reflect God.

📖 Read Genesis 6:12–13. What impact did man's reign have on the earth?

_____

_____

_____

In Genesis 3 and in the chapters following, Adam did not succeed in fulfilling God's desires or obeying God's directions. He sinned and brought death into the world (Romans 5:12–21). He began to show forth his own image, a fallen, self-centered, selfish image (Genesis 5:3). The fruit he bore in children and in his own character reflected this fallen image. Genesis 6:5 reveals the condition of man. Instead of reigning over life, man was enslaved to his selfish, sinful desires. Man was doing a poor job of cultivating life and guarding what he had been given. Instead of nurturing and growing life in goodness and purity, man had "corrupted" life (Genesis 6:12). Instead of guarding life from harm, violence "filled the earth" (Genesis 6:13).

There was no oneness—with God or with one another. Therefore, God destroyed all life except for Noah, his family, and the creatures in the Ark (Genesis 7—8). But God was not through with man or His creation, and as we will see in Day Three, we find Adam mentioned again in the New Testament.

The Scriptures declare that *"all have sinned."* Everyone has a nature of sin, a tendency to choose what I want rather than what God wants. After all, "I" is the middle letter in "sin." The choices every person has made throughout history, since Adam made his choice, have proven this diagnosis to be true. Romans 5:12 says it plainly, *"all . . . sinned."* The description of man in Scripture bears this out. Men are dead in trespasses and sins, sons of disobedience, living in the lusts of the flesh, indulging the desires of the flesh, children of wrath, separated from Christ, without God, without hope . . . and the list could go on. True, some people appear to be very nice and make law-abiding choices, but no one chooses God's will with every choice or considers pleasing God each moment of their day—and anything short of this is wickedness before God. Some have very "respectable" flesh; others live in the gutters of society. Either way, all have sinned and all are accountable to a righteous and just God. As a result, all are dying. First Corinthians 15:22 says it plainly, *"in Adam all die."*

How can man get out of this dead-end condition? How can man once again walk in oneness with God the way God desires? Man's condition is such that only God can provide the solution.

Man's Condition and God's Solution: The Last Adam

As we have seen, Adam did not succeed in fulfilling God's design for him, nor did his children. How was man to fulfill God's design and purpose? How could the shattered oneness be rebuilt? God called many to follow Him and worked in their lives in amazing ways. Perhaps man could will himself back into obedience. Think of Abraham, Isaac, Jacob and his twelve sons (the nation of Israel). God gave them His Law through Moses, and Israel promised to keep it. But they could not. They became idolatrous. God sent many prophets to proclaim His Word and His way. Yet still mankind fell short of the image of God. Man's condition required redemption. He needed a Savior—not just to pay for his failure, but to rebuild what had been destroyed. God promised a Redeemer would come, and in the fullness of time He sent His Son, the Lord Jesus Christ, the last Adam (Romans 5:14; 1 Corinthians 15:45; Galatians 4:4–5). In a tangible sense, Christ is God's provision to recreate His image in us.

Doctrine
THE LAST ADAM

God promised a Redeemer would come, the Seed of the woman, and in the fulness of time He sent His Son, the Lord Jesus Christ. He was the Seed born of a woman and the Last Adam (Galatians 4:4; 1 Chronicles 15:45).

📖 Read John 1:14–17. Who is the Word?

_____

📖 Read John 1:1–5. Why do you think John calls Jesus "the Word"?

_____
_____
_____

According to verses 3–5, what did Jesus do?

_____
_____
_____

And in verse 14, what did He do?

_____
_____

John calls Jesus "the Word" because Jesus perfectly expressed (communicated) who God is, because He is God. He created all things. In the fullness of time He became flesh (a man), the God-Man. As such He revealed the glory of God to men. The Apostle John was an eyewitness to this (see also 1 John 1:1–3).

As God, Jesus was able to walk in oneness with the Father, here on the earth, just as Adam did in the garden before he sinned. There has always been a oneness between God the Father and Jesus the Word because the Word is God. The Scriptures tell us that Jesus came and lived the perfect life: a life that perfectly reflected the image of God, that perfectly reproduced the fruit of an obedient life, and that showed forth the ability to reign with perfect righteousness.

In addition to demonstrating that oneness with God is possible, Jesus had another reason for becoming flesh. He knew that because of Adam's choice, sin and death passed on to all mankind (Romans 5). He knew that all mankind needed a way out of their desperate condition because their life was lacking God. His purpose and work, therefore, included restoring us to oneness with God.

📖 Read the following passages. In the space provided, briefly describe why Jesus came.

John 10:9 _____

_____

John 10:10 _____

_____

John 10:11 _____

_____

John 10:17–18 _____

_____

Jesus came not to be served but to serve and to willingly lay down His life as a ransom for sinners (see Matt. 20:28; Mark 10:45).

Jesus came not to be served but to serve and to willingly lay down His life as a ransom for sinners. He was willing to be lifted up on a Roman cross and die so that any "*sheep*" who would "*come through Me*" could "*be saved*." He came that we "*might have life, and . . . have it abundantly*." He paid the price for man's disobedience and sin. He died in our place so we could know His life.

The Bible tells us that Jesus did not come just to reveal the perfect image of God, to reproduce the perfect fruit of an obedient life, or to show forth the ability to reign with perfect righteousness. **He Came to Restore!** He came to accomplish our redemption and restoration. He came to restore the oneness that sin had shattered. This was accomplished through Christ's crucifixion and resurrection and ultimately through our glorification.

📖 What prophecy concerning Jesus do you find in Matthew 1:20–21?

_____

_____

_____

Jesus was delivered up to be crucified because of our transgressions—our choices to go our own way, to step aside from the path God has commanded. Jesus was born to die for our sins. His death provided for our justification. His resurrection showed that we were justified in God's sight. Christ's death perfectly paid the penalty for our transgressions against God and His holy nature, character, and work. The angel told Joseph in Matthew 1:21 that the name of the baby to be born to Mary would be "*Jesus*" because He would "*save His people from their sins.*" Jesus is the Greek equivalent of the Hebrew name, Joshua, which means "The Lord [*Yahweh*] is salvation."

📖 For what kind of people does Romans 5:6–10 tell us Jesus died?

_____

_____

_____

Jesus came to die for those who were "*helpless*" (5:6). The word means "without strength," the idea being one who is sick, diseased, or weak to the point that one cannot stand.

Romans 5:6 also says we were "*ungodly*," those without proper reverence for God. This word refers to those who by their own personal choice refuse to worship God as He deserves or as His Word reveals. It is not giving God what is rightly due to Him—due reverence, respect, and pure worship (in spirit and in truth). The "*ungodly*" are those without the fear of God, without reverence for God. As a result, they worship false gods, including themselves, and false concepts of who they think God is. All of that is an abomination to God and unacceptable, but Jesus died for the ungodly.

He also came to die for "*sinners*" (5:8), those who always come short of God's goal of a pure, righteous life. They are like an archer who always comes short of the target, never reaching the standard God requires.

Jesus came to die for the "*enemies*" of God (5:10). This refers to those who "*walk according to the flesh*," who "*set their minds on the things of the flesh*" (Romans 8:4–7). That means anyone who chooses to measure life by his own fleshly, self-centered, self-approved standards. "*The mind set on the flesh is hostile toward God,*" meaning that as an enemy of God he will not follow the will of God as given in His Word (Romans 8:7–8).

 Do you see yourself in any of these descriptions now or in the past?

_____

_____

In Acts 2, Peter preached about the salvation Jesus brought. He spoke first of the forgiveness of sins and second about the coming and indwelling of the Holy Spirit of God. In Jesus' short lifetime, He fulfilled the desires and purposes of the Father. After He revealed to the disciples that He would be going away from them, Jesus also told them that He would send "another" (one of the same kind) that would be a "Helper" to them (John 14:16). The Holy Spirit's indwelling of us brings us life and restores the oneness God designed us for (John 14:16–17).

Christ's death, burial, and resurrection took away the penalty and the power of sin and gave us His holy and powerful life in the Person of the Holy Spirit

> **"For while we were still helpless, at the right time Christ died for the ungodly."**
> **Romans 5:6**

within us. He gave His life *for* us so that He could give His life *to* us: to live *in* us that we might live *through* Him. His life is one with the Father, and because we now have His life in us (the Holy Spirit), we can begin to reflect the image of God. We can walk in oneness with our Creator who is also Lord and Creator of His new creation, and by our submission to Him, He can reign through us.

Because of Jesus Christ, what can our daily life now look like? What kind of people are we now able to be? How can we actually live the life that reflects Him as He designed?

ONENESS BETWEEN ME AND GOD

God's design—how do we experience it? How can we personally know and experience this forgiveness and life, this restoration to fellowship and oneness? There is a statement that is sometimes quoted when one thinks of the ways of God and how He communicates with man: God does not say seven different things. He says one thing seven different ways. That is true when it comes to describing the restored walk of oneness between man and the Lord.

The Bible uses several pictures of a man who has chosen to follow God, the man who has given his life to Jesus Christ and been reconciled to his Creator and Lord. As you examine these pictures, ask yourself if they are descriptive of you and your life right now.

The Scripture speaks of:

✓ A child coming forth from his mother's womb, being born from above by the Spirit of God (John 3:3–8).

✓ Having a new nature because God's *"seed abides in"* us (1 John 3:9).

✓ Being adopted into the family of the Father and looking forward to an inheritance (Romans 8:15–17; Ephesians 1:5–6).

✓ Coming out of the dominion of Satan and darkness into the kingdom of the Beloved Son, the Lord Jesus (Acts 26:18; Colossians 1:13–14).

✓ Being like a slave set free because the *"redemption"* price has been paid (Romans 3:21–26; Ephesians 1:7).

✓ A man in Christ being a *"new creature"* or new creation (2 Corinthians 5:17).

✓ Being made alive together with Christ (Ephesians 2:5).

In each of these pictures, we see a common thread: change of life. When a person chooses to accept Christ as their Savior, they become a new person. Second Corinthians 5:17 states it clearly: *"If any man is in Christ, he is a new creature; the old things passed away; behold, new things have come."*

The following pictures describe the lifelong walk with Christ that results:

✓ Walking in the light as He is in the light and enjoying fellowship with the Father and the Son (1 John 1:3–7).

Jesus gave His life for us so that He could give His life to us: to live in us that we might live through Him.

✓ Abiding in the Vine, the Lord Jesus, and bearing much fruit (John 15).

✓ Following Jesus as a sheep follows a shepherd (John 10:27–29).

✓ Living a life of dying—taking up one's cross daily, choosing to follow God rather than our own way (Luke 9:23–25).

✓ Walking *"with all humility and gentleness, with patience, showing forbearance to one another in love"* (Ephesians 4:2).

✓ Being called the dwelling place of the Holy Spirit, the picture of God's presence with the children of Israel in the Holy of Holies (1 Corinthians 6:19–20; 2 Corinthians 6:16–18; 7:1).

✓ Being filled with the Spirit, the perfect picture of oneness—God residing in man, empowering and directing his life (Ephesians 5:18–21).

APPLY Look back through these pictures. What are some thoughts that come to mind which best describe how a Christian's life should be characterized? (For example, "a child coming forth from his mother's womb" might bring to mind total dependence, bonding, intimacy, or love.)

_____

_____

_____

_____

_____

_____

_____

Now think about yourself. Are these some of the same characteristics that can be used to describe your life?

_____

_____

_____

_____

In each of the pictures of a person's relationship to God there is an essential oneness marked by a full, vibrant life. Each one is characterized by freedom and joy—a life that truly glorifies and magnifies the Lord Jesus Christ.

📖 Read Galatians 5:22–23. According to this passage, how should a Christian's life be characterized?

_____

_____

_____

_____

> *We were made to walk in oneness with God.*

> *"The fruit of the Spirit is love, joy, peace, patience, kindness, goodness, faithfulness, gentleness, self-control."*
> *Galatians 5:22–23a*

Think how wonderful relationships would be if the fruit of the Spirit were evident 100 percent of the time!

A Christian's life should be characterized by the fruit of the Spirit. This includes *"love, joy, peace, patience, kindness, goodness, faithfulness, gentleness,* [and] *self-control."* In other words, when the Spirit of God is in control of our lives, He bears the fruit of God's image in us—He reflects God in us! Think of all the relationships you have and how perfect they would be if the fruit of the Spirit were clearly evident 100% of the time in you and in them. This will only be possible when we have been freed from the presence of sin—that is, when we get to heaven. But as believers, we have already been freed from the penalty of sin—the eternal condemnation of hell (Romans 5:9). And, as we grow in dependence and submission, we experience an ever-increasing freedom from the power of sin because Christ left His Spirit who dwells within us (*"greater is He who is in you than he who is in the world"* 1 John 4:4).

Does this mean that when I become a Christian, I will never sin again? No, but when you become a Christian, then Christ, through the Person of the Holy Spirit, comes to live in you—takes up residence in you (Ephesians 3:17). Our "flesh" (the sin propensity we are born with because of Adam's sin) is still present in our lives even after we become a Christian. However, its power over us has been neutralized (Romans 6:5–7, 11–13). As believers, we now have the power to choose right over wrong because we have the indwelling sufficiency of Christ within us (Ephesians 3:16).

📖 Write out beside each of the following verses what you discover about our freedom over the power of sin and where we get that power:

Romans 6:6 _____

_____

Romans 6:22 _____

_____

Romans 8:3–4 _____

_____

Romans 13:14 _____

_____

Galatians 5:16 _____

_____

Galatians 5:24–25 _____

_____

When we choose to submit to God and His will, then He will reflect Himself in us (1 John 1:6). Remember that Adam's choice to disobey God is what caused both his need for a Savior and our own. God has made the necessary provision for us to reflect Him through the giving of the Holy Spirit. Before we came to know Christ, we had no power over sin—we were slaves to sin. Now, we have been enslaved to God. We do not have to live in sin (choosing our own way over His) because we walk according to the Spirit.

We are able to do this by "putting on" the Lord Jesus (this has the meaning of wearing Christ like a garment) which gives no room for our "flesh" and its lusts. When faced with the choice, we have to aggressively "kill" our sinful desires and passions. Finally, Paul exhorts us and the Galatians that if we have the Spirit within us, we should walk in His strength, not our own. When the Spirit of God is in control of our lives, we again reflect God's image. Our actions and attitudes in our relationships with others demonstrate the fruit of the Spirit.

Romans 8:1–30 gives an overall picture of God's purpose for His Spirit to dwell in the believer. He wants to . . .

✓ guide our daily walk,

✓ enable us to have a walk of life and peace,

✓ empower us to live in righteous harmony with God,

✓ lead us to guard against the control of our sinful "flesh,"

✓ help us grow in practical righteousness (yielding the members of our bodies to God as instruments of righteousness—see also Romans 6:12–13, 17–23),

✓ prepare us for the redemption of our bodies,

✓ help us in prayer,

✓ ultimately, to fulfill God's purpose for us in conforming us to the image of His Son, and

✓ show us the security of the love God has for us.

📖 Read Romans 8:29. Before Adam was even created, what had God purposed for His children?

_____

_____

_____

God's eternal purpose for all of His children is to ". . . *become conformed to the image of His Son.*" He has "*predestined*" that all who know Him will reach this goal when they are glorified. Philippians 1:6 states it this way: "*He who began a good work in you will perfect it until the day of Christ Jesus.*" God is going to keep working on us until we go to be with Him. Second Corinthians 3:18 says that "*. . . we all, with unveiled face beholding as in a mirror the glory of the Lord, are being transformed into the same image from glory to glory. . . .*" In other words, the more we see of God, the more we are changed to be like Him, bit by bit. God is in the process of re-creating His image in us through the Lord Jesus.

We were designed to reflect God, knowing Him in an intimate oneness. Our Lord went to the cross to reveal the holiness and love of His Father. He made full provision for us to know God in His forgiveness with no barriers between us and Him. As a result, the Father will have many sons, all glorified—walking in the glory of God, in perfect harmony with Him, always pleasing Him, with no barriers or walls, only peace and fullness of joy. Consequently, we are able to know His life, a life of full fellowship and peace with no division or strife.

God is going to keep working in our lives until we go to be with Him.

FOR ME TO FOLLOW GOD

God's original design was "*very good*" (Genesis 1:31). Adam and Eve were to walk in perfect oneness with God: glorifying Him by reflecting His image, reproducing His image, and reigning in life in a way that reflects His image. But then sin came into the picture, and its effect is still with us today.

📖 Read Romans 5:15 and 1 Corinthians 15:22. Through whom did sin enter the world?

_____

What was the result of Adam's sin?

_____

Who has sinned since then?

_____

Have you ever sinned?

_____

Adam sinned, and because of him, all men are sinners. Have you ever sinned? Of course you have. We all have because we all have a nature of sin. And sin bears consequences.

Looking back at Day 2, what did Adam lose when he sinned?

_____

_____

_____

_____

Adam lost many things, but the one that mattered the most was the oneness and harmony that he experienced with God. When Adam passed his sin to us, he passed his loss of oneness to us as well.

Read Romans 6:23. What are the wages (payment) for sin?

_____

Read Galatians 6:8. What shall "*the one who sows to his own flesh*" reap?

_____

But what about "*the one that sows to the Spirit?*"

_____

The penalty for sin is clearly stated—it is death and corruption. Sin results in both physical death and spiritual death (i.e., separation from God, a lack of oneness). But sin also corrupts our physical bodies, our spiritual well-being, our families, and our world. But there is a way out, an escape! Jesus paid the penalty. He took your place on the cross so that you can be reconciled to God.

Because Adam's sin has been passed to us, we have the same need to have oneness with God reestablished.

📖 Read Romans 5:8. Who did Christ die for?

_____

Why would He do such a thing?

_____

📖 Read Romans 6:23 again. It says that *"the wages of sin is death."* What then, will you be able to expect by surrendering to Jesus Christ as your Lord?

_____

So, do you know Him—are you a new creature? Has your life ever been changed by choosing to live for Christ?

📖 Read 2 Corinthians 5:17. What happens to you when you give yourself to Christ?

_____

📖 Read 2 Corinthians 5:15. Based on this verse, what do you think verse 17 means by *"in Christ?"*

_____

Being *"in Christ"* is at the heart of oneness. It means that we are no longer to live for ourselves, but for Jesus Christ—to follow God.

If you've never given your life to Jesus Christ, ask Him to come into your life and dwell in your heart now. Begin your journey of following God. You will be able to depend upon the Creator of the universe for guidance in all that you do.

 Open your heart to Him and pray where you are:

✓ Admit that you have sinned, that you are not walking in step with God, not pleasing Him nor glorifying Him in your life.

✓ Repent of that sin—change your mind, turn to God, and turn away from sin—and by faith receive His forgiveness based upon His death on the cross for you.

✓ Open your life to receive Him as your living, resurrected Lord and Savior. He has promised to come and indwell you by His Spirit and live in you as the Savior and Master of your life.

✓ He wants to live His life through you—conforming you to His image, bearing His fruit through you and giving you power to reign in life.

Come to Him now. In your own words, simply tell Him you want to know Him personally, and you willingly repent of your sin and receive His forgiveness and His life. Tell Him that you want to follow Him forever. Welcome to the family of God and the greatest journey of all.

If you think you've been a Christian for years, and yet this sounds foreign to you, please ask God to reveal your own heart to you. Perhaps you've always known so much of Jesus that you've missed a personal relationship with Him altogether.

Fellowship with God comes in knowing Jesus as Savior and following Him as Lord.

If you have made that choice, stop now and thank Him for His mercy and grace in bringing you out of a hopeless existence into life—joy with God forever. If you have made that choice, you have the strength and power of the Holy Spirit within you to walk in harmony with God. Is your life daily characterized by surrender just as it was at the point of your salvation?

_____

Harmony with God only occurs as we walk in surrender to Him.

A mark of spiritual maturity is how quickly we recognize our sin and turn to God in repentance, surrendering our life to Him (our will, our agenda, and our desires). In Him, you have everything you need to be everything God calls you to be. Are you choosing to walk in harmony with Him? This harmony with God only occurs when we make the choice to surrender to Him.

Are you choosing to submit to His authority? This is how you walk in the Spirit. And as you walk in the Spirit, your life exhibits the fruit of His life in you. Your relationships with God and others are strengthened because your life is now characterized by love, joy, peace, patience, kindness, goodness, faithfulness, gentleness, and self-control.

Spend some time in prayer with the Lord right now.

 O God, I begin to see what You intended my life to be, and I see how very short I have fallen of that mark. I am humbled that You would daily seek such an intimate relationship with me. Teach me each morning to abide in Christ so that I may guard all You have seen fit to give me. I would walk each day in oneness with You, that my life may be marked by humble obedience, loving service, and the fruit of Your Spirit. In Christ's sufficiency, Amen.

Write out your prayer to the Lord. Seek His presence in your life and His power to be what He would have you be.

_____
_____
_____
_____
_____
_____
_____
_____
_____
_____

Notes

Notes

Following God in Reverence and Obedience

ebrews 11:7 offers us this commentary on Noah: *"By faith Noah, being warned by God about things not yet seen, in reverence prepared an ark for the salvation of his household, by which he condemned the world, and became an heir of the righteousness which is according to faith."* As we will see this week, Noah was not a perfect man, but he revered God, and out of that reverence flowed obedience. Out of Noah's obedience came Noah's stake in the righteousness of faith. It really is a remarkable thought that it is not my good moral behavior that shapes my righteousness, but my faith—my willingness to trust God and take Him at His word. Imagine the cost of this faith for Noah. For one hundred years he and his sons faithfully worked on building an ark for the coming flood. Imagine the mocking of neighbors as he constructed this boat miles from any water. Imagine their sneers as he spoke of judgment coming through rain—something the people had never seen. But Noah revered God, so he took Him at His word. What God said He would do, He would do. What God said would happen, really would happen.

It is not my good moral behavior that shapes my righteousness, but my faith—my willingness to trust God and take Him at His word.

Where Does He Fit?

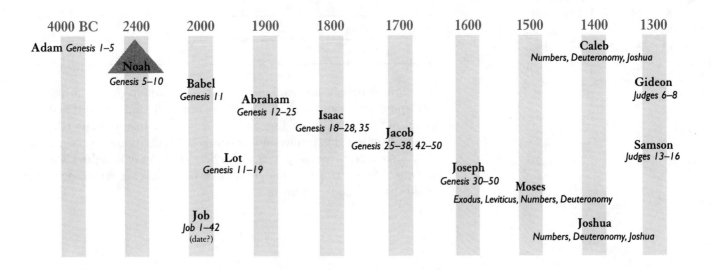

BLAMELESS IN HIS DAY

The world of Noah's day was flooded with evil. Sin had its corrupting influence on ancient society. Wickedness had left its stain. And God said, "Enough!"—

The LORD saw that the wickedness of man was great on the earth, and that every intent of the thoughts of his heart was only evil continually. And the LORD was sorry that He had made man on the earth, and He was grieved in His heart. And the LORD said, 'I will blot out man whom I have created . . . for I am sorry that I have made them.'

It was a dismal time for creation. In the midst of all that wickedness, only Noah was a man who *"found favor in the eyes of the LORD."* We are told that Noah *". . . was a righteous man, blameless in his time,"* and that he *"walked with God."* Today we want to look at the covenant God made with Noah to see what we can learn about reverence and obedience.

📖 Read Genesis 6:1–7, 11–12. Identify and list four reasons the Scripture gives for God judging the ancient world.

_____

_____

_____

_____

The first reason given here for God's judgment is that *"the wickedness of man was great on the earth."* This focuses on the actions of man's life. Second, not only were man's actions wicked, but his attitudes were also. Verse 5 indicates that *"every intent of the thoughts of his heart was only evil continually."* There was nothing good in man. What a tragic commentary that the Lord was sorry that He had made man, and He was grieved literally to the core of His being. We see from verses 11–12 that the earth was *"filled with violence"* and that all flesh had *"corrupted their way upon the earth."*

📖 Look again at Genesis 6:7. What does God's judgment include?

_____

_____

_____

_____

God didn't judge simply mankind, but all of creation from man to animals to creeping insects and birds. Some believe our entire universe suffered cataclysm in God's judgment. Romans 8:19–22 reveals that in man's fall, creation was subjected to futility and was enslaved to corruption. Verse 22 tells us, *". . . the whole creation groans and suffers the pains of childbirth together until now."* Since creation is under the curse of sin, it is not surprising that it would share in God's judgment.

Did You Know?

WHO WERE THE "SONS OF GOD" WHO COHABITED WITH THE DAUGHTERS OF MEN?

Theologians are divided on this issue. Some believe this refers to angels taking human wives. But this would seem to be impossible since angels are called "ministering spirits." A spirit could not have relations with a human. Most likely *"sons of God"* points to the godly line of the descendants of Seth, who after a time, took unbelieving wives from out of the line of Cain, and godly values were lost. This would be the first example of believers being unequally yoked with unbelievers.

📖 We are told in verse 8 that Noah *"found favor in the eyes of the Lord."* But why? Read chapter 6, paying close attention to verse 9, and list all the reasons Noah and his family were spared.

_____

_____

_____

We see in verse 9 that Noah is called *"a righteous* [honest with other men and obedient to the laws of God] *man, blameless in his time,"* and that he *"...walked with God."* When Scripture says that Noah was *"blameless"* that does not mean that he was sinless. In fact, the statement, *"blameless in his time"* seems to suggest blameless in a relative sense (compared to the sinful people around him). But though he was not perfect, as later chapters make clear, he walked with God. That is what God desires from us as well. A less obvious reason Noah was spared was because he was obedient. God gave Noah warning, but unless Noah built the ark in obedience, he would not have been spared.

God looked down and saw Noah and liked what He saw. Noah stood out from all the people around him. As God looks at you, do you blend in with everyone around you, or do you stand out as someone who seeks to find favor in His sight? Many times we worry more about how well we fit in with the people around us than we do with seeking God's favor through an attitude of reverence and obedience.

 APPLY Take an honest look at your life. Where do you think you are?

Blending In ◄━━━━━━━━━━━━━━━━━━━━━► Standing Out

NOT DELIVERED FROM THE TROUBLE, BUT THROUGH IT

Quite often we look to God for deliverance from trouble, yet that is not always His way. Sometimes God determines that He can get greater glory by safely bringing us through trouble rather than avoiding it. Noah spent one hundred years of labor preparing the ark and one year living on it. Then he came out to a world that had to be completely rebuilt. God's deliverance for Noah didn't mean that he had no troubles, but that he had God's faithful provision in all of his troubles.

God instructs Noah to build an *"ark,"* and gives the measurements in cubits. A cubit was the length from the elbow to the tip of the finger (roughly 18 inches).

📖 Read Genesis 6:13–16. What dimensions does God give for the ark?

_____

_____

_____

God's deliverance for Noah didn't mean that he had no troubles, but that he had God's faithful provision in all of his troubles.

What other details does God specify in verse 16?

_____

_____

_____

_____

Did You Know?
THE ARK

Gopherwood, or cypress wood, was later used by the Phoenicians for shipbuilding because of its lightness and durability.

Scholars estimate that less than half of the space provided on the ark would be needed to house the 17,600 species of animals found on the planet today.

The ark was essentially a large rectangle, something like a shoe box, made of gopherwood. It was three levels high, with each level being about 15 feet tall, and a window/door on the side near the top. Its carrying capacity equaled that of 522 standard railroad stock cars (each of which can hold 240 sheep).

📖 Read Genesis 6:17—7:1. What did God instruct Noah to do?

_____

_____

_____

_____

What did God say that He would do?

_____

_____

_____

_____

God tells Noah **1)** to build the ark, **2)** to load the animals, **3)** to store food for his family and the animals, and **4)** to get on board. It is interesting that as we compare his task concerning the animals with that of the food, different terminology is used. Noah is instructed to "*bring*" two of every kind of animal on the ark, but he is also instructed to "*take*" and to "*gather*" the food for himself. Did he have to gather the animals, or simply load them? The answer is in 7:9, "*. . . there went into the ark **to Noah** by twos, male and female, as God had commanded Noah*" (emphasis added). For Noah and his sons to collect a pair of each of the animals was an impossibility. A team of thousands would have taken years to accomplish that task. Chapter 6, verse 20 also states, "*. . . two of every kind shall come to you . . .*" indicating that God brought the animals to Noah supernaturally.

APPLY Can you remember a time in your life when God gave you what seemed like an impossible task? What was your response?

_____

_____

_____

Often in following God we worry and waste time trying to do what only God can do, while neglecting specific areas (attitudes, relationships, responsibilities) that *are* under our control. Where God guides, He provides—either by giving us the tools we need to accomplish the task, or by taking care of those things Himself. He will do one or the other!

📖 Read Genesis 7:10–24 carefully.

When did the flood begin?

_____

_____

How long did it rain?

_____

Who and what were saved from the flood?

_____

_____

_____

Who shut the door of the ark?

_____

How high did the water rise?

_____

What all died due to the flood?

_____

How long did the flood last?

_____

After seven days of silence, the thunderclouds burst forth (7:10) and rain began to fall. At the same time, the "... *fountains of the great deep burst open* ..." indicating that water was coming from the ground as well as the sky (7:11). Though all the text tells us is that the water *"increased greatly"* (7:18), our knowledge from science of the power of moving water tells us that this was not benign like the gradual filling of a pool. This flooding left destruction in its wake, so that *"all flesh that moved on the earth perished ... of all that was on the dry land"* (7:21–22). By this flood, the Lord *"blotted out every living thing that was upon the face of the land"* (7:23).

The world of the past was very different from the world we know today. The archeologist and the theologian agree on this. Not only were there many more kinds of plants and animals, but the biblical record indicates that man's life span was significantly longer prior to the flood. After the flood, man's protein needs were greater, and at God's instruction he ceased to be a vegetarian (Genesis 9:3).

Until the judgment of Noah's time, rain had never been known. Genesis 2:6 tells us that *"... a mist used to rise from the earth and water the whole surface of the ground."* Many creation scientists think that prior to the flood the earth was enveloped with a dense vapor canopy of atmospheric moisture. The results of such a canopy would be a greenhouse environment with high humidity and a universally warm climate (something the fossil record indicates was true of the past). This would explain where enough water came from to rain constantly for forty days and nights.

Did You Know?

WERE THERE DINOSAURS ON THE ARK?

That dinosaurs existed is evident from the fossil record. But when they existed is unclear, as is the question of when they died out. In several places the Bible gives descriptions of what appear to be dinosaurs, and most likely they died out in conjunction with the flood. Most dinosaurs were herb eaters, and one can easily understand their role in creation when the population of man was too small to cultivate the whole earth. Probably the climactic changes of the post-flood world insured their extinction.

God does not always deliver us from trouble; sometimes He delivers us in the midst of it.

Those who have experienced a localized flood can begin to appreciate the catastrophe of a global flood. Disaster and chaos covered the earth. Scientists believe that with the flooding there was also massive volcanic activity and geological disturbance. Though Noah was protected from harm in this flood, he did not escape it. God took him through the flood. God does not always deliver us from trouble; sometimes He delivers us in the midst of it. God's deliverance for Noah didn't mean that he had no troubles, but that he had God's faithful provision in the midst of his troubles.

APPLY Can you think of a time when you were surprised by a trial because you expected God to deliver you from having to go through it and He didn't?

_____

_____

_____

_____

Looking back, can you see ways the Lord enabled you to walk through the trial instead of around it?

_____

_____

_____

 *Noah* DAY THREE

A NEW WORLD ON THE OTHER SIDE

"But God remembered Noah. . . ."
Genesis 8:1

Chapter 8 begins with these words: *"But God remembered Noah. . . ."* Sometimes we feel abandoned when God allows us to go through a hard time. We are tempted to think God has forgotten us. But from Noah we learn that we are never forgotten. The Lord *"remembered"* Noah, and on the other side of the trial, a new world was waiting. It was a different world from the one Noah had known. Though sin had been judged by the flood, it had not been completely removed, but the world Noah found was better than the one he left. If, as 2 Peter 2:8 tells us, Lot's soul was *"tormented day after day"* by the lawless deeds of Sodom, we can assume Noah felt the same torment in the wicked days in which he lived. After the flood, that overt wickedness was gone. It was a new world on the other side of his trial. And, that is the way it is when God brings us through the fire. Today, as we look at Noah after the flood, let's see what we can learn about the fruit of obeying God.

📖 Take a moment to read through Genesis chapter 8. What does Noah do as recorded in verse 20?

_____

_____

_____

_____

📖 Read Genesis 7:2. Why would God have told Noah to bring more of the clean animals than the unclean?

_____

_____

_____

_____

Although there is no record of God instructing Noah to build an altar and make sacrifices, God had made provision for this by having Noah bring seven each of the *"clean"* animals. In fact, verse 20 is the first mention in all of Scripture of an altar being built. On the other side of the flood was a new level of worship for Noah.

📖 Now look at Genesis 8:21–22. What three promises does God make in response to Noah's worship?

_____

_____

_____

God was pleased with Noah's offerings. As a result, God promises to Himself that first, He will never again curse the ground or secondly, destroy every living thing on account of man. Third, God promises that as long as the earth remains, the seasons and night and day will continue. Some see a scientific significance to this first mention of seasons. If the pre-flood earth was in fact, surrounded by a vapor canopy, there would have been no seasonal change. Much like a cloudy night keeps temperatures warm, while a clear night is much cooler, this canopy would have held in the sun's warmth and distributed it evenly around the planet. After this canopy was removed, seasons would then be possible.

📖 Read Genesis 1:28 and Genesis 9:1. What similarities do you see?

_____

_____

_____

In Genesis 9:1 we see the same responsibility given to Noah that was given to Adam and Eve. God has begun again, and with Noah and his family has made a fresh start for man. But His plan for man has not changed.

📖 Read Genesis 9:8–17. With whom did God establish the covenant?

_____

_____

_____

_____

What was God's part in the covenant?

_____

_____

_____

Did You Know?
THE NOAHIC COVENANT

Throughout the Old Testament God made covenants with men, including Abraham, Israel (Jacob), Moses and David. But the covenant with Noah was the very first.

What was Noah's part in the covenant?

_____

What was the sign of His covenant?

_____

This covenant is to Noah, his sons, his descendants, and *"every beast of the earth."* God promises that He will never again destroy the whole earth with a flood. Verse 12 tells us it is for *"all succeeding generations,"* and this idea is further clarified in verse 16 where the Lord calls it an *"everlasting covenant between God and every living creature."* God required nothing of Noah in this covenant. The covenant was in no way dependent upon anything that he did or did not do. The rainbow is the sign of the covenant, standing as a constant reminder of God's promise. We can imagine the emotions Noah and his family felt the first time a storm brewed after the flood. They would have no way to know that this storm would not be the judgment that the first was. What comfort they must have taken from seeing the rainbow and remembering the promise!

Noah DAY FOUR

EVEN THE RIGHTEOUS STUMBLE

It is the man who allows his past victories to fool him into thinking he stands who is most vulnerable to falling.

Though Noah was called a *"righteous man"* and *"blameless in his day,"* this didn't make him immune to temptation or unable to sin. Often we think just because someone trusts God in one area they can't fall in another. But James 3:2 reminds us, *"we all stumble in many ways,"* and Paul instructed us in Romans 3:23, *"for all have sinned and fall short of the glory of God."* It is the one who allows his past victories to fool him into thinking he stands who is most vulnerable to falling. Sadly, it is after our greatest victories and triumphs that we are most susceptible to sin. Today we will look at a tragic chapter in Noah's life, and hopefully through his example guard ourselves from the same mistakes.

📖 Read Genesis 9:18–19. What do you learn?

_____

_____

_____

In these verses we see that it was from the three sons of Noah that the earth was repopulated. It is interesting that Ham's son is named Canaan. Most likely the land of Canaan was populated by his descendants. As we see later, God plans that those who will follow Him will one day conquer Canaan and subjugate its people. Joshua led Israel into the Promised Land for this very purpose.

📖 Read verses 20–21. What did Noah do, and what happened as a result?

_____

_____

_____

Not only is Noah the first man in the Bible to build an altar, he is also the first mentioned in the Bible to discover wine and get drunk. As a result of his drunkenness, his guard was let down, and he behaved lewdly. When we are controlled by alcohol, we do things we normally would not do. The fruit of the Spirit is self-control—the fruit of alcohol is a lack of control.

📖 Read Genesis 9:21–29. Why do you think Noah cursed Canaan?

_____

_____

_____

_____

The fact that Noah *"uncovered himself"* implies more than simple nakedness. In other words, it is likely that one of Noah's sons did more than merely see his father's nakedness. The Hebrew word means "shameful nakedness" and is associated with immoral behavior. It is different from the word that simply means to be naked.

The curse makes it clear that there were actions. When 9:24 speaks of the *"youngest son,"* it doesn't mean Ham, for Japheth was the youngest of Noah's immediate sons. It literally reads, "youngest one" and should be taken to mean his youngest descendant, which apparently was Canaan. The judgment is pronounced because of something Canaan *"had done to him."* Apparently Canaan took advantage of his grandfather's drunken state and committed some immoral act with him.

This sad and tragic incident is the last narrative we find of Noah's life and the only record of the three hundred and fifty years he lived after the flood. Genesis 9:28–29 simply informs us that Noah died. This tainted account of Noah's latter years stand as a warning to each of us not to try and live on past laurels of faithfulness. There are many more who start strong in the Christian life than there are who finish strong.

 As you follow God, do you find yourself closer to God in times of trial or in times of comparative ease?

_____

If you find yourself relaxing your guard when not in a trial, what can you do to protect yourself during those times?

_____

_____

_____

Perhaps the most important lesson from Noah is to not be surprised at our own failures and to be watchful against them. Noah didn't fall during his adversity but during his ease. We see this pattern throughout Scripture. David fell with Bathsheba when he took a vacation from the war. Although our flesh wants life to be easy, easy isn't always best. Times of ease are not to be avoided, but they are also not times to let down our guard.

Noah's latter years stand as a warning to each of us not to try to live on past laurels of faithfulness. There are many more who start strong in the Christian life than there are who finish strong.

FOR ME TO FOLLOW GOD

I t is unfortunate that Noah's life ended on such a negative note, for in his day, he walked with God like none around him. But we must recognize that God wants us to see both sides of Noah. He does not want us to put the saints of old up on a pedestal where we cannot relate to their lives. The narrative of Noah, like all the Patriarchs, is given for our instruction so that we may learn from their lives. If we will look closely at the life of Noah we can learn both from his successes and from his failures. If we are wise, we will learn from his life.

Review Genesis 6:9. What did God say is the reason that Noah found favor in His sight?

_____

_____

_____

Look back at Day One and define in your own words what each of the following mean (i.e., what it means to find favor in God's sight):

righteous

_____

blameless

_____

walk with God

_____

Noah wasn't sinless, yet he found favor in God's sight. How? By having a proper view of God which resulted in a life characterized by reverence and obedience.

 Take an honest look at your life. Put an X in the place on the line that characterizes your level of obedience in the following circumstances.

Trials and Temptations

My Way ⟷ God's Way

Peace and Prosperity

My Way ⟷ God's Way

How do we learn to walk in consistent obedience with God, God's way, without continually wandering away on our own paths? Obedience comes from having a proper view of God, and a proper view of God comes from knowing Him. When we know God, our desire to obey comes from our desire to please Him—because of who He is. The more we desire to please Him, the easier it becomes to recognize God working. As we learn to recognize His hand, we willingly yield, because of love, to whatever trial or prosperity He may be taking us through.

> *"By faith Noah, being warned by God about things not yet seen, in reverence prepared an ark for the salvation of his household, by which he condemned the world, and became heir of the righteousness which is according to faith."*
>
> *Hebrews 11:7*

How do we get to know God? How did you get to know your spouse or best friend? By spending time with them. God is not trying to hide Himself from us. He wants us to know Him and has given us that ability through:

- ✓ free access to Him through prayer, and
- ✓ the revelation of His Word.

Do you consistently take advantage of God's open invitation into the throne room of the KING OF KINGS, LORD OF LORDS, GOD ALMIGHTY, THE CREATOR, THE GREAT I AM? Do you consistently take advantage of His Word and get to know Him as your **Shepherd, Comforter, Peace,** and **Rest.**

If this hunger is not in your heart, ask Him to create it within you. He wants you to know Him.

Spend some time in prayer with the Lord right now.

O God, I have tasted Your goodness, and it has both satisfied me and made me thirsty for more. I am painfully conscious of my need for further grace. I am ashamed of my lack of desire. O God, the triune God, I want to want You; I long to be filled with longing; I thirst to be made more thirsty still. Show me Your glory, I pray, so that I may know You indeed. Begin, in mercy, a new work of love within me. Say to my soul, "Rise up, my love, my fair one, and come away." Then give me grace to rise and follow You up from this misty lowland where I have wandered so long. In Jesus' name. Amen.

A. W. Tozer

Write out your prayer. Tell Him you want to know Him more. Ask Him to increase that desire within you.

_____

_____

_____

_____

_____

_____

_____

_____

_____

_____

_____

Notes

TRUSTING GOD'S SOVEREIGNTY

Everyone has heard of the trials of Job. Perhaps no biblical story has had a broader secular audience than the story of Satan's attacks on this righteous man. In fact, the book of Job was probably the first book of the Bible ever written. Although the book of Genesis records events that happened earlier, they were written later as God related those events to Moses.

The narrative of Job's trials contains all the elements of great drama: tragic circumstances and supernatural difficulties, false accusations, abandonment by loved ones, all culminating in a radically altered perspective on life. Few of us will encounter the depth of difficulty Job faced, but the lessons he learned are the same lessons each of us must apply in our own adversities. Someone once said, "*major* surgery is when it is *me* being operated on." Our trials and tribulations may not seem major to someone else, but they are major to us as we seek to follow God through them.

> *Either every event in life is under the scrutiny and scope of God's reign or nothing is. There is no such thing as partial sovereignty.*

WHERE DOES HE FIT?

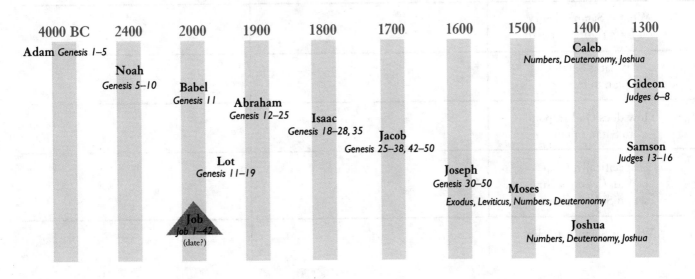

STANDING IN THE CROSSHAIRS OF THE ENEMY

"*There was a man in the Land of Uz, whose name was Job.*" Our story begins with the introduction of a man who is set apart in his day. He was a righteous man who went through tremendous trials; yet, the Scripture records that he came to know God in a new way in them.

📖 Read Job 1:1. What four things do you learn about Job's character at the outset?

_____

_____

_____

_____

The very first verse gives us four descriptions which underscore Job's uniqueness: **1)** he was blameless (no fault could be found in examining his life), **2)** he was upright (his character was predictably good), **3)** he feared God (a heart reverence), and **4)** he turned away from evil (he made right choices). We also see in Job 1:3 that he was the wealthiest man in the East. But as we will see in today's lesson, Satan sought to undermine his life.

📖 In identifying the parameters of Job's trials, it is important that we understand the roles of the participants. Read through Job chapters 1 and 2, and use what you learn to fill in the chart below.

Questions	Job 1:6–22	Job 2:1–10
Where does Satan encounter the Lord?		
Who brings up Job in the conversation?		
What is Satan's theory on Job's righteousness?		
What is Satan's plan to test it?		
How does God respond to Satan's plan?		
Specifically, what boundaries does God set on Satan's attack?		
What is Satan's attack?		

Questions	Job 1:6–22	Job 2:1–10
How does Job respond?		
Who does Job realize is in control of his misfortune?		
What do you think these encounters teach about Satan's relationship to God?		

It is interesting that Satan shows up in Job's life at the invitation of God. Satan goes to God with the other angels, and God asks, *"Have you considered My servant Job?"* God brings it up. Satan replies, "Yes, he blesses you, but only because you are blessing him—take that away, and he'll curse you." God grants Satan permission to attack, but in each case, He sets boundaries on how far Satan can go. First, he can only touch Job's possessions, but it doesn't work. Job still blesses God. Then Satan is allowed to touch Job's health, but not to take his life. It still doesn't work. Job doesn't sin—nor does he get mad at the devil. He always gives God credit, acknowledging His sovereignty. Job evidently understood that Satan is under God's authority.

 What difficulties have you recently experienced? Write them below.

Things which seem good that God has taken away:

_____

_____

_____

_____

Things which seem bad that God has given:

_____

_____

_____

_____

If you are serious about trusting God's sovereignty, you need to respond to these things in the same way that Job did. In Job chapter 1, when God had taken away all of Job's possessions and all of his children, he responded by saying, *"The LORD gave and the LORD has taken away. Blessed be the name of the LORD."*

 Take a few minutes in prayer and "bless" the name of the Lord. Thank Him for what He has given, and bless Him in what He has taken away. This choice of the will may not be what you are feeling, but if you obey, the feelings *will* follow.

> ## Job was "blameless and upright, fearing God and turning away from evil," yet God allowed affliction in his life.

In Job chapter 2, when God had given the adversity of sores covering his body, Job's wife advised him to *"curse God and die."* But he responded in faith, asking, *"Shall we indeed accept good from God and not accept adversity?"* Take a few minutes in prayer and "accept" your adversity from the Lord. Again, you may not feel like it, but if you act in faith, the feelings will come in due time.

In both chapters we see that *"in all this Job did not sin with his lips"* nor did he blame God. Maybe in your own trials the same cannot be said. If you sense God convicting you of sinning with what you say about Him or by blaming Him, write down what you have done, and then repent of it.

It will be helpful to keep these things in mind as you seek to apply what you are learning this week.

Job **DAY TWO**

WITH "FRIENDS" LIKE THESE...

Job has just been blasted with a barrage of adversity to which most of us, thankfully, cannot relate. In one day all of his oxen and donkeys were stolen by a marauding band of Sabeans, fire from God consumed all his sheep, the Chaldeans robbed him of all his camels, and all his sons and daughters were killed in an accident. All but four of his servants perished in the various catastrophes. To make matters worse, his good health was taken from him, as he was afflicted with sore boils from the soles of his feet to the crown of his head. But his trials are not limited to the loss of his family, possessions, and health. Today we want to examine the spill-over of his trials into his relationships.

📖 Read Job 2:9. What does Job's wife say to him?

_____

_____

What do you think she meant by her comments?

_____

_____

_____

"CURSE GOD AND DIE"

It was usual among the heathen, when disappointed in the results of their prayers and offerings to their gods, to turn to cursing the gods. Perhaps there is also the suggestion that if a god, so cursed, is angered, perhaps he will kill the worshiper and put him out of his misery.

Job's wife, the "God-given helpmate," questions, *"Do you still hold fast your integrity?"* In essence, she is asking "Are you still trying to maintain this facade that this trial is not God's retribution because of your sins?" Her advice to him is to, *"Curse God and die!"* It was usual among the heathen, when disappointed in the results of their prayers and offerings to their gods, to turn to cursing the gods. Perhaps there is also in this the suggestion that if a god, so cursed, is angered, perhaps he will kill the worshiper and put him out of his misery.

📖 How does Job respond to the worldly advice of his wife, and what is his reasoning for embracing the difficulties (2:10)?

_____

_____

Job tells his wife that she speaks as a fool. His logic is impeccable: "How can we accept blessings from the Lord and then refuse to accept adversity?" If God really is the sovereign, omnipotent Creator of all, then certainly He is responsible for the misfortunes that come our way. Even if God does not personally dole out our miseries, He shares partial responsibility for them inasmuch as He has the power to prevent them and chooses not to exercise that power.

Word quickly spread of Job's ill fortune, and three different friends journeyed to him. Job's three friends are to be applauded that for the first seven days with him they said nothing, ministering to their comrade only by their presence. Yet when they did speak, their words were hardly comforting.

📖 Take a few minutes to read the passages below. Summarize in a sentence or two the perspective of each of his friends.

Eliphaz (Job 4:1–9)

_____

_____

Bildad (Job 8:1–22)

_____

_____

Zophar (Job 11:1–20)

_____

_____

Eliphaz' main point is summarized in Job 4:8, "*. . . those who plow iniquity and sow trouble harvest it.*" In other words, Job must be reaping what he has sown. Bildad seems to be on the same wavelength. In Job 8:6 he responds to Job's question from the end of chapter 7 (If I have sinned, why doesn't God pardon?) by saying, "If you would seek God and implore the compassions of the Almighty [implying that Job has not done this] then God will restore you." Zophar completes the trilogy. He clearly does not believe Job's protests of innocence. In Job 11:13 he states, "*If you would direct your heart right . . .*" indicating this is something he believes Job has not done. His closing contrast in verse 20 seems to convey where he thinks Job is: "*But the eyes of the wicked will fail, and there will be no escape for them; And their hope is to breathe their last.*"

Fundamentally, what do you think is wrong with these three responses?

_____

_____

_____

Before we are too quick to condemn Job's friends, we must recognize that we have the advantage of having God's perspective laid before us. Were we in their shoes, we would perhaps be prone to make equally wrong assumptions. In them, we see the folly of us all when we judge one another without all the facts. Rightly does Job rebuke them: "*Sorry comforters are you all. Is there no limit to your windy words?*" (Job 16:2b–3a).

"*. . . Shall we indeed accept good from God and not accept adversity?*"

Job 2:10

Extra Mile
JOB'S FRIENDS

Read the following chapters, outlining the advice of Job's friends and his responses to them. Write down the essence of each argument and response.

Job 4—5 (Eliphaz)

Job 6—7 (Job)

Job 8 (Bildad)

Job 9—10 (Job)

Job 11 (Zophar)

Job 12—14 (Job)

Job 15 (Eliphaz)

Job 16—17 (Job)

Job 18 (Bildad)

Job 19 (Job)

Job 20 (Zophar)

Job 21 (Job)

Job 22 (Eliphaz)

Job 23—24 (Job)

Job 25 (Bildad)

Job 26—31 (Job)

List all the ways in chapter 31 in which Job claims to have been faithful. What can you conclude that each man thinks about God?

Job's friends and family tried to comfort him, but they misunderstood what God was doing. Have you ever said the wrong thing trying to comfort someone because you thought you knew what God was up to?

_____

_____

_____

_____

Maybe you need to go to someone and make things right. If so, don't delay.

Job DAY THREE

THE DANGER OF SELF-JUSTIFICATION

Job's continuing debate with his three friends goes nowhere. But in chapter 32 a new friend comes on the scene named Elihu. At first he is reticent to enter into the fray, out of respect for Job's older friends have more wisdom and more right to express it. But eventually he speaks up because of his anger towards Job justifying himself before God (32:2), and towards the three friends *"because they had found no answer, and yet had condemned Job"* (32:3). Though he is but a youth, we will see from his speech that he has more wisdom than all the other friends combined. Today we want to focus on the rebuke of Elihu to see what spiritual wisdom we can glean. Today's homework will be more time-consuming, but it will be worthwhile.

Read Job chapters 32—37. (Reading these five chapters will take a while, but really is necessary to get the big picture of what Elihu has to say.) Summarize what you learn from the key verses listed.

Job 33:13

_____

_____

Elihu states, *"Why do you complain against Him, that He does not give an account of all His doings?"* In other words, "What right do you have to demand an explanation from God?"

Job 34:10–12

_____

_____

_____

> *". . . Far be it from God to do wicked-ness, and from the Almighty to do wrong."*
>
> **Job 34:10**

Here we read, *". . . Far be it from God to do wickedness, and from the Almighty to do wrong."* God is good. That is fundamental to any question we may have of Him. Whatever He does, we know that His action (or inaction) is not wicked or wrong no matter how it may look to us.

Job 35:2

_____

_____

_____

"Do you say, 'My righteousness is more than God's'?" Whenever we sit in judgment on the actions of God, we place ourselves above Him.

Job 37:14–24

_____

_____

_____

Elihu closes his arguments with a stern reminder of the greatness of God and the inappropriateness of man questioning God. We all need to be reminded of these truths.

📖 Take some time to read Job chapters 38—41. Here, we see God's response to Job. Summarize God's reply (40:8).

_____

_____

_____

The statement in Job 40:8 speaks volumes about what really is taking place when we refuse to trust God's sovereignty in the midst of hard times. When we grumble and complain about our circumstances, we are discrediting the judgment of God. We are condemning Him so that we may be justified. Because God is sovereign, any griping about what He allows into our lives is, in reality, an accusation that He is mismanaging our lives. This doesn't mean that we have to deny the pain, nor that we cannot express our pain to Him; what it means is that we must trust God in the midst of it.

In 1 Corinthians 10:13 we are told, *"No temptation has overtaken you but such as is common to man; and God is faithful, who will not allow you to be tempted beyond what you are able, but with the temptation will provide the way of escape also, that you may be able to endure it."* Every "trial" (same root Greek word as *"temptation"*) that comes our way, God faithfully filters. Then His faithfulness places before us the way to endure it. We can trust His sovereignty.

🛑 APPLY Job was blameless in causing his trials, but he was wrong in how he responded when his trials continued. Have you grown impatient with the trials God has allowed to continue in your life? If so, why?

_____

_____

_____

_____

If so, you are by your actions accusing God of mismanaging your life. You need to confess this to your Heavenly Father, and ask Him to help you trust Him.

> **"Will you really annul My judgment? Will you condemn Me that you may be justified?"**
>
> **Job 40:8**

A NEW VIEW OF GOD

On the other side of his trial, Job has a new view of God and a new view of his life. What a message of hope that is! Whatever our difficulty we can know that someday it will come to an end, and it will have been worth it that we followed God. The apostle Paul was no stranger to adversity. He spent years in prison on false charges. He was beaten *"times without number"* (2 Corinthians 11:23). He was often in danger of death. Five times he received from the Jews thirty-nine lashes with the whip. Three times he was beaten with rods. Once he was stoned and left for dead. Three times he was shipwrecked, and on one of those occasions he spent a night and a day treading water. His whole life as a believer was characterized by danger. (See 2 Corinthians 11:23–32.) Yet, he wrote in 2 Corinthians 4:17, *"For momentary, light affliction is producing for us an eternal weight of glory far beyond all comparison."* In his mind, whatever difficulty God allowed him to go through was unworthy of comparison with the joys of following God. He had learned that on the other side of adversity is a new view of God.

📖 Today we want to focus on the things Job learned. This, it would seem, was God's purpose for the trials. Look at Job 42:1–6, and make a list of each thing Job confesses to God.

42:1–2

_____

_____

42:3

_____

_____

42:4

_____

_____

42:6

_____

_____

> **"I know that Thou canst do all things, And that no purpose of Thine can be thwarted."**
> **Job 42:2**

Job begins in 42:1–2 by affirming the character of God (*"Thou canst do all things, And no purpose of Thine can be thwarted"*), and by so doing, confesses his wrong thinking about God. Job had slipped into the wrong view that God must not have been powerful enough to prevent his suffering, and that the adversity which came Job's way was not what God had purposed. In verse 3, Job confesses that he had spoken about things he didn't really understand. In Job 42:4, he switches from defending himself before God, which he did earlier, to asking God to instruct him. What an example for every believer! In our adversities we should be asking God what He wants to teach us. Instead, we spin our wheels trying to determine whether or not the calamity is fair. In verse 5 Job admits that his understanding of God was hearsay before, but is now personal experience. In verse 6 he closes out his response by confessing that his new view of God has humbled him.

📖 What is God's verdict on the counsel of Job's friends according to Job 42:7?

_____

_____

_____

God's wrath was kindled against Job's friends because they had *"not spoken of Me what is right."* How often, like Job's friends, our uninformed opinions misrepresent God.

📖 What was the outcome of Job's trial according to chapter 42, verses 9–17?

_____

_____

_____

_____

_____

We see that Job was accepted by the Lord (v. 9), and that all of his fortunes were restored *"twofold."* Some would argue that his possessions were doubly restored except his children. If you think about it though, Job had seven more sons and three more daughters. Job would be reunited with the other ten children in heaven.

APPLY Think about the last big trial you went through as a Christian. Did you learn new things about the Lord? Did you grow in your faith? Remembering these things may give you needed encouragement in your present and future trials. Write out some things that God taught you about Himself during this trial.

_____

_____

_____

_____

Most of us will never encounter tragedy on the level that Job endured. But each of us will find difficulties of our own, and to us they will be significant. There are no immunization shots to protect us from difficulty. But there is God's sovereignty to filter that difficulty and to guide us through it.

In James 1:2 we are instructed, *"consider it all joy . . . when you encounter various trials."* The word "various" there means "multi-colored" or "multi-faceted." In other words, our trials all come in different shapes and sizes—no two are alike. In Ephesians 3:10, Paul uses this same Greek word to describe *"the manifold wisdom of God,"* and in 1 Peter 4:10, Peter uses the same Greek word to speak of *"the manifold grace of God."* Although our trials come in different shapes and sizes, God's grace and wisdom do too. It is as if He takes a scoop and measures out our trial, then takes the same scoop to measure out corresponding wisdom and grace sufficient for our need. God sovereignly rules over all our trials.

In our adversities we should be asking God what He wants to teach us. Instead, we spin our wheels trying to determine whether or not the calamity is fair.

FOR ME TO FOLLOW GOD

Job was *"blameless and upright, fearing God and turning away from evil,"* yet God allowed affliction in his life. That one truth makes it clear that following God does not mean that we will have no difficulties. We see from the first two chapters of Job that our difficulties lie in two different directions. Some of our difficulties are the result of God taking something away from us that we want and like. Others are a result of God giving us something we don't want or like.

📖 Summarize Job's trials from chapters 1 and 2.

_____

_____

_____

_____

_____

Who was ultimately in control of Job's trials? (Circle the appropriate answer.)

    a. Job
    b. Satan
    c. God

APPLY   Right now, all of us are either in the midst of a trial, coming out of one, or about to go into one. Describe the trial(s) in your life right now.

_____

_____

_____

Who is ultimately in control of your trials? (Circle the appropriate answer.)

    a. You
    b. Satan
    c. God

Which of the following best describes you?

    ____ I never worry about anything.
    ____ I continually worry about the results of the decisions I make.
    ____ I am constantly anxious about the well-being of my loved ones.
    ____ I instinctively attempt to fix everything.
    ____ I have a tendency to feel sorry for myself.
    ____ I am learning to daily trust God with everything in my life.
    ____ I often feel overwhelmed by my circumstances, but I am trying to seek God in them anyway.

📖 Read the following verses, and write down what each one tells you about God's purpose for trials in your life.

> *The most important realization that we can make in the midst of a trial is that whatever the secondary causes are, ultimately God is sovereign over it.*

Romans 8:28–29

_____

_____

James 1:2–4

_____

_____

2 Corinthians 4:7–10

_____

_____

_____

2 Corinthians 4:17

_____

_____

God's ultimate purpose in each of our lives is to conform us to the image of Jesus Christ. To that end, He uses trials in our lives to create endurance, perfecting and completing us, that we may be lacking in nothing. We see our own weakness in trials so that we may know that the power in our lives is not of ourselves, but of God. And in our weakness, the life of Jesus may be clearly seen for His eternal glory.

Where do you begin? With . . .

- ✓ Learning God's character by saturating your mind in God's Word,
- ✓ Humbling yourself before Him in prayer through every circumstance.
- ✓ Walking daily in the realization that God is sovereignly in control and that His purpose is your greatest good.

Are you following God in the midst of your trials?

Spend some time in prayer to the Lord right now.

O God, be exalted over my possessions. Nothing of earth's treasures shall seem dear to me if only You are glorified in my life. Be exalted over my friendships. I am determined that You shall be above all, though I must stand deserted and alone in the midst of the earth. Be exalted above my comforts. Though it mean the loss of bodily comforts and the carrying of heavy crosses, I shall keep my vow made this day before You. Be exalted over my reputation. Make me ambitious to please You even if as a result I must sink into obscurity and my name be forgotten as a dream. Rise, O Lord, into Your proper place of honor, above my ambitions, above my likes and dislikes, above my family, my health and even my life itself. Let me decrease that You may increase; let me sink that You may rise above. In Jesus' name, Amen.

A. W. Tozer

> *"Consider it all joy, my brethren, when you encounter various trials, knowing that the testing of your faith produces endurance. And let endurance have its perfect result, that you may be perfect and complete, lacking in nothing."*
> **James 1:2–4**

Write out your prayer. Remind yourself that He is always sovereign and worthy to be praised. Ask Him to give you a new view of Himself and of yourself.

_____

_____

_____

_____

_____

_____

_____

_____

_____

_____

Notes

Notes

Abraham

FOLLOWING GOD AT ANY COST

The lives of the people of God from the Old Testament speak volumes on what it means to follow God. One principle we see repeated in one person after another is that God initiates our pursuit of Him. The lives of saint after saint reveal the reality of *"the word of the LORD"* coming to give direction and vision. God has a purpose for every life, and He places within each heart a vision or a sense of that purpose, that design He has for them. But it is not enough just to know the will of God, we must also walk in the way of God: God's will, God's way.

As we enter the world and walk of Abraham, we will see the methods and mistakes as he follows the plan of God. Like so many others, his is an imperfect pursuit. And yet God used him mightily and made Abraham the father of many nations. In fact, God promises that in him all the nations of the earth are blessed. Whenever we follow God, we become useable by Him as an agent of blessing. But God must do His work in us before He can ever do a work through us. We will see this truth lived out in Abraham.

> **God must do His work in us before He can ever do a work through us.**

WHERE DOES HE FIT?

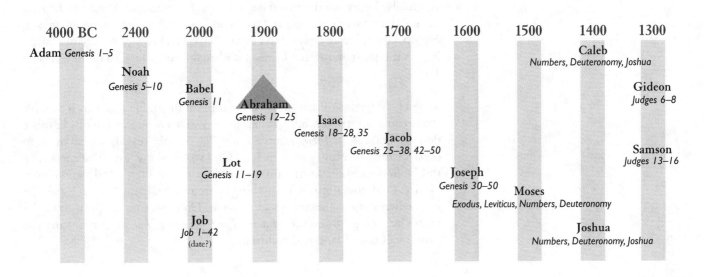

4000 BC	2400	2000	1900	1800	1700	1600	1500	1400	1300

Adam *Genesis 1–5*

Noah *Genesis 5–10*

Babel *Genesis 11*

Abraham *Genesis 12–25*

Isaac *Genesis 18–28, 35*

Jacob *Genesis 25–38, 42–50*

Lot *Genesis 11–19*

Joseph *Genesis 30–50*

Job *Job 1–42* (date?)

Moses *Exodus, Leviticus, Numbers, Deuteronomy*

Caleb *Numbers, Deuteronomy, Joshua*

Gideon *Judges 6–8*

Samson *Judges 13–16*

Joshua *Numbers, Deuteronomy, Joshua*

THE VISION OF GOD

The curtain rises on Abraham's life in the pagan land of Ur of the Chaldeans (modern day Iraq). One would look in vain for an explanation of why he was selected for God's purposes. The only answer we have is that by grace, God sought him out. God had a unique purpose for Abraham's life. He called him from a pagan culture to make a new nation—one that would follow God. We know nothing of his life before God called him, yet through him the nation of Israel was born, and all the nations of the earth were blessed. Abraham, then named Abram, left Ur at God's initiation, and what family he had went with him. Joining in the journey were his father (his mother was apparently dead), his wife Sarai, and his nephew Lot (whom his father was raising after the death of Haran, Abraham's brother). Though Abraham had some idea of what God was doing, it was unclear as to exactly when and how this would be realized. He knew enough to point his sails in the right direction, but there would be a lot of waiting and trusting before God's plan for his life became a reality, and there would be mistakes along the way.

📖 Read Genesis 12:1–3. What would it cost Abraham to follow God's direction?

_____

_____

_____

_____

If he obeys, what does God promise him?

_____

_____

_____

> One would look in vain for an explanation of why Abraham was selected for God's purpose. The only answer we have is that by grace, God sought him out.

God's vision for Abraham is only partially revealed here. He calls him to leave **1)** his country, **2)** his relatives, and **3)** his father's house (his inheritance). God does not tell Abraham exactly where he is going, but He does promise to make of him a great nation and name, and through him to bring blessing to all the families of the earth. This giving of the vision in Genesis 12 is actually the second time God has revealed His intent to Abraham. In Acts 7:2 we learn that God appeared to Abraham the first time while he was in Mesopotamia, **before** he lived in Haran. This explains why Abraham's father begins the journey toward Canaan and makes it as far as Haran (Genesis 11:31).

When God begins to paint His vision for Abraham, He first fills it in with the broadest of strokes, but with each successive encounter He fills in more details. The call in Mesopotamia (Acts 7:2–5) only reveals Abraham is to depart from his country into the land God would show him. The encounter in Haran (Gen. 12) adds the promise of blessing and fame and nationhood. Notice, God does not reveal anything more to Abraham until he leaves Ur in obedience. Once he arrives in Canaan, God gives more specifics to the vision by saying *"to your descendants I will give this land,"* incorporating the promise of both a land and children.

As the story of Abraham's life continues to unfold, we see a detour along the way.

📖 Read through Genesis 12. In light of the promises God has given Abraham, what is significant about Abraham's deception concerning Sarah in Egypt?

_____

_____

_____

_____

_____

Remember, God has promised Abraham offspring (which requires he have a wife). But rather than trust that where God guides, He provides, Abraham trusts his own striving (v. 13) to secure his safety and that of his wife. It is also significant that Egypt was the first place on his journey where he did not build an altar. There is no mention of his seeking God again until he comes back to the altar he had built between Bethel and Ai (13:4).

Once Abraham returns to the promised land and begins to seek the LORD, there is more revelation of God's plan.

📖 Read Genesis 13:14–17, and answer the following questions.

What land was going to be his?

_____

_____

To whom does God promise the land?

_____

_____

How long will the land be theirs?

_____

How many of Abraham's descendants will there be?

_____

_____

Once Abraham separates from Lot, God reveals again His intent to give to Abraham's descendants the promised land of Canaan. To this vision the LORD adds the facts that it will belong to his descendants forever and that God will make his descendants as numerous as the dust of the earth.

As we see God's plan for Abraham's life, the "vision" is a progressive revelation. It is not given in one big package. It is more like a scroll, unrolling a bit every day.

Did You Know?

WAS ABRAHAM AN ISRAELITE OR A JEW?

He was neither. Abraham's grandson Jacob was renamed "Israel" by the Lord. The descendants of Jacob's twelve sons became the twelve tribes of Israel which made up the nation. The term "Jew" was a designation originally associated with the tribe of Judah, from which the Messiah would come, and eventually broadened to include all Israelites. Abraham *was* referred to as a "Hebrew," a designation possibly referring to "the one who crossed the river," that is, the Euphrates.

📖 Read Genesis 15, and identify the additional details God reveals of His plan for Abraham.

_____

_____

_____

_____

_____

_____

_____

To the promise is added that Abraham's descendants will not be through a relative, but through his own body, and will outnumber the stars. In verse 18 God even adds a boundary to His promise: from the Nile to the Euphrates. It is worth noting that in Genesis 14:21–24 Abraham refuses the gift from the king of Sodom, wanting to make certain that his prosperity could only be attributed to God. When God promises that Abraham's reward will be great, it would seem that He is honoring the heart Abraham showed to the king of Sodom.

📖 Why, according to 15:1–6, does God say Abraham is reckoned righteous?

_____

The text makes it clear that all Abraham did was believe that what God said in verses 1–5 was true. Biblical faith is simply taking God at His word, believing that He will do what He promises. The word *"reckoned"* basically means that it was "credited to his account." For a more detailed consideration of this word "reckoned," see Romans 4.

APPLY God had a specific purpose for Abraham's life. Perhaps your purpose is not so dramatic as establishing a new nation, but God *has* a specific purpose for you. Maybe it means raising godly children or becoming a foreign missionary or teaching a Bible study, or maybe He hasn't fully revealed it yet. Think about your life, and list any details God has revealed thus far.

_____

_____

_____

_____

Have you been fully obedient to "the vision" that God has revealed to you thus far? We see from Abraham's life that normally God does not reveal the next step until we have obeyed the steps He *has* revealed. Write down any action you need to take in obedience.

_____

_____

_____

_____

"... then he believed in the LORD; and He reckoned it to him as righteousness."
Genesis 15:6

Biblical faith is simply taking God at His word, believing that He will do what He promises.

God's Will, but Not God's Way

It was God who sought out Abraham in Ur of the Chaldeans. It was God who kept seeking Abraham. It was God who had a plan for Abraham's life. Abraham's part was to trust God—to take Him at His word. It is in the arena of trust where we see Abraham's humanness. He wanted to believe, but he struggled with balancing trust in God with taking matters into his own hands. In Egypt we saw his trust slip a bit. In Genesis 16 we see that, though Abraham believed that God would fulfill His promise, he again took matters into his own hands. God had promised a son, but nothing had yet happened. The biological clock was ticking. Sarai (Sarah) then came up with an idea of how they could help God's plan along: Abraham would conceive a child with her Egyptian maid. Sarai's suggestion was an accepted practice of the culture of the day according to documents of antiquity that have been discovered, but it was not God's way.

📖 Read Genesis 16:1–3. To whom is Abraham listening?

_____

Who do you think Abraham is depending upon for God's promises (offspring) to be fulfilled?

_____

Verse 2 says, *". . . and Abram* [Abraham] *listened to the voice of Sarai."* It seems painfully obvious that because Abraham's focus is on his circumstances instead of God, he does not yet recognize that it is God who will fulfill the promise, not him. He is striving to fulfill God's promise in human strength. We do the same thing when we use the world's methods to try to help God out.

Abraham sleeps with Hagar, and she becomes pregnant. The child born to Hagar was Ishmael, who is claimed by most Arabs as their forefather.

📖 Read Genesis 16:12, and write down the prophecy concerning Ishmael.

_____

_____

_____

_____

God reveals that Ishmael will be a *"wild donkey of a man"* and his hand will be against everyone, and theirs against him. It is also predicted that he will live to the east of his brothers. This Hebrew phrase may be taken literally, or could also mean that he will live in defiance to his brothers. Both are true, for not only do the Arabs live to the east of Israel, but the hostility between the two groups continues even today.

APPLY Do you ever find yourself anxious about the fulfillment of God's purpose in your life?

☐ Yes ☐ No

AN EGYPTIAN MAID

When Abram and Sarai were unsuccessful in having children, Sarai suggested Abram use her maid, Hagar, as a surrogate mother. This maid was apparently part of the wealth that Abram and Sarai brought back from their ill-fated journey to Egypt. Not only was the maid Egyptian, but the idea may have been as well. It was an accepted cultural practice although clearly not the will of God.

Trusting God is not characterized by anxiety. Anxiety is a warning sign that you are depending on yourself or circumstances rather than God to accomplish His purpose.

When you're faced with fear or anxiety, how should you respond? (Check all that apply.)

____ by helping God out with His plan by trying to fix it
____ by going before God in prayer and waiting for His guidance
____ by trusting God that He is in control
____ by seeking God in His Word
____ by following someone else's plan that seemed to work
____ by seeking wise, godly counsel and filtering it through God's Word

God wants us to give our fears to Him and trust Him with those things we are anxious about, realizing that He is in control. His Word gives us truth concerning our circumstances and guidance for our daily lives. At times, God uses the body of Christ (other believers) to come alongside us and help us get a glimpse of His perspective.

Whenever we try to help God out, we do more damage than good. In Galatians 4:23 the apostle Paul states that Ishmael was *"born according to the flesh,"* while Isaac was born *"through the promise."* In Galatians 4:29 he is even more specific and states that Isaac was *"born according to the Spirit."* The fruit of Abraham's striving did not bring blessing; it only brought a strife that existed in Paul's day (Galatians 4:29) and continues today.

> **God wants us to give our fears to Him and trust Him with those things we are anxious about, realizing that He is in control.**

Abraham DAY THREE

GOD'S WILL, GOD'S WAY

For thirteen years after the birth of Ishmael, Abraham heard nothing from God. The heavens were silent. But finally God broke the silence when Abraham was ninety-nine years old. Not only did God restate His promise, but He changed Abram's name to Abraham. The name Abram literally means "exalted father" which must have been painful to a man who was childless until he was eighty-six. And then he had to live with the shame of his fleshly mistake with Ishmael. But God not only renewed the vision, He enlarged it. The name Abraham means "father of a great multitude." Again we see a bit more added to Abraham's understanding of God's plan for his life.

📖 Read Genesis 17. Look for *new* details of the vision God reveals to Abraham in this passage.

How does God further clarify His promises concerning Abraham's descendants (vv. 4–6)?

_____

_____

_____

_____

What does God now require of Abraham as a sign of the covenant (vv. 11, 14)?

_____

_____

What does God say about Sarah (vv. 15–16)?

_____

_____

_____

What does God say about Isaac (vv. 19, 21)?

_____

_____

_____

_____

What about Ishmael (v. 20)?

_____

_____

_____

Now, instead of making Abraham only a *"great nation,"* God promised he would be the father of *"a multitude of nations."* He promised to be God to him and his descendants and to give him a son from Sarah. God also promised that Sarah would be a mother of nations, making it clear that the multitude of nations comes through Isaac, not Ishmael. He also promised Abraham that kings would come forth from him (which they did: David, Solomon, Christ). Lastly, God promised that the covenant would be fulfilled through Isaac.

📖 What is Abraham's initial response to the news of the coming son (vv. 17–18)?

_____

_____

_____

Why do you think Abraham would respond this way?

_____

_____

_____

When God spoke of the coming son there is no mention of Ishmael. At a glance it seems that Abraham did the right thing. Verse 17 tells us, *"Then Abraham fell on his face"*—and that is what he should have done—when God speaks to any individual, the appropriate thing for that person to do is to fall on his face in worship. But notice something else here—Abraham fell upon his face and laughed. He said in his heart, "Will a man that is one hundred years old bear a child, and will a woman that is ninety years old bear a child?" **He laughed**—"That's impossible, God! It will never work! Let me suggest a more sensible way—*'Oh that Ishmael might live before Thee!'"*

Abraham's laughter was not of joy but of doubt, for he still wanted the promise to be fulfilled in Ishmael. With all the benefit of hindsight, it is easy to wonder at Abraham's unwillingness to take God at His word, but if we place ourselves in his shoes it is easy to see us doing the same thing.

📖 Once it is clear to Abraham what God intends to do, how does he respond (vv. 23–27)?

_____

_____

Abraham obeyed the requirements of the covenant God was making. It is significant that verses 23 and 26 indicate Abraham performed the circumcisions *"the very same day."* His faith is expressed by immediate obedience as ours should be. Delayed obedience often becomes disobedience. Perhaps a less obvious aspect of Abraham's obedience is the fact that he had relations with his wife Sarah as soon as he recovered from the circumcision, for three months later she becomes pregnant (see vv. 17:21; 21:2).

There is one final incident to look at today. You will remember from Day Two's study that the catalyst for the mistake of Ishmael was Abraham listening *"to the voice of Sarai."*

📖 Read Genesis 21:1–14. What does Sarah ask Abraham to do (v. 10)?

_____

_____

What do you observe has changed about Abraham's response to her?

_____

_____

Sarah wants Abraham to turn Ishmael and Hagar out, but instead of acting on what Sarah says, he hesitates. He has learned from his mistake of chapter 16. Abraham does not dismiss what Sarah says, but wants to make sure he follows God. In Abraham's distress, God meets with him and reassures him.

Abraham learned his lesson from the mistake of Ishmael. After that we see him pursuing God's will in *God's* way.

> *Whatever God's will is for us, He wants it done His way so that He will get all the glory. For that to be a reality, we sometimes have to lay our vision on the altar and put it to death.*

Abraham DAY FOUR

THE SACRIFICE OF FAITH

There is a process at work in Abraham's life that is often repeated in the lives of those who would follow God. God has birthed a vision in his heart and has allowed Abraham to make mistakes as he tries to realize the vision in his own way. Now God is going to put the vision to death and then resurrect it. In so doing, God is working so that there will be no doubt in Abraham's mind that God, and not he, is making the vision a reality. Whatever God's will is for us, He wants it done His way so that He will get all the glory. For that to be a reality, we sometimes have to lay our vision on the altar and put it to death.

📖 The whole of Abraham's vision is wrapped up in his son, Isaac, who is now somewhere between thirteen and twenty years old. Read through Genesis 22:1–2, and write down exactly what God asks Abraham to do.

_____

_____

_____

_____

God tells Abraham to take his only son (this is how God sees it, for Isaac is the only son of Abraham and Sarah—both possessors of the promise according to Genesis 17:16–17) and to sacrifice him as a burnt offering on Mount Moriah. This would be a difficult request of any parent, especially parents who had waited so long for a child. But this was no ordinary child. He was the child of promise through whom the whole world was to be blessed. Abraham was not simply asked to give up his son, but his whole life's vision as well.

📖 Look at Genesis 22:3–5. As they are journeying to the mountain, what two things does Abraham tell his servants that he and Isaac are going to do?

_____

_____

How do you think Abraham could say these things?

_____

_____

_____

Abraham tells his servants two important things: **1)** what he and Isaac will do is an act of worship, and **2)** they will both come back. He doesn't know how they will both come back, but he is confident they will. Abraham understands that his obedience to God is his means of worship, and it is significant that this is the first time the word worship appears in the Bible.

What does Isaac ask his father in verse 7?

_____

_____

And how does Abraham respond to Isaac (v. 8)?

_____

_____

What does this reveal about where Abraham has placed his trust?

_____

_____

Abraham's answer is *"God will provide for Himself the lamb for the burnt offering, my son."* Again we see that the focus of Abraham's trust is no longer himself, but God. He doesn't worry about *how* God will do what He intends; he simply trusts that He *will* do what He intends.

📖 **Doctrine**
ISAAC AS A TYPE OF CHRIST

Isaac may be one of the most complete Old Testament types of Christ. The *"only son"* of his father, he apparently did not resist his own sacrifice and carried the wood on which he was to be offered up the mountain. God's last minute replacement of Isaac with the sacrificial ram is a beautiful picture of Christ's substitutionary atonement—He suffered the death that was to be ours.

📖 In Genesis 22:9–10, God tells us what happened next. And, in Hebrews 11:17–19, He tells us what was going through Abraham's mind. According to these verses, how could Abraham offer his own son to be sacrificed?

_____

_____

Here we see that offering Isaac was an act of faith on Abraham's part. Abraham has finally learned that it is God's job to accomplish His vision. He fully expects that even if he kills Isaac, God is able to raise him from the dead. Whether God resurrects Isaac or does something else, Abraham has full confidence that God will bring the promise to pass. How God would do it was God's problem to worry about, not Abraham's.

📖 Read Genesis 22:11–12. What does Abraham's obedience reveal about his heart?

_____

_____

_____

In verse 12, God says, *"Now I know that you fear God, since you have not withheld your son, your only son, from Me."* Abraham's obedience in doing what God had asked, though it seemed to make no sense and conflict with the vision, proved that God was more important to him than the vision, embodied in Isaac. It reflected a heart willing to please God no matter what the cost, and a willingness to trust God to do what only He could do.

APPLY Sometimes God calls us to die to the vision He has given us. Look back to Day One and remind yourself of the vision God has given you thus far. Are there any "Isaacs" in your life that you need to lay on the altar. Have you willingly given your desires for the fulfillment of the vision over to God?

_____

_____

_____

God births the vision, then He kills the vision, then He resurrects it in such a way that all can see that what happens is His work, not man's.

The example of Abraham and Isaac is consistent with how God has dealt with His saints throughout the ages. God births the vision, then He kills the vision, then He resurrects it in such a way that all can see that whatever happens is His work, not man's.

We can see this principle of the death of a vision illustrated in the life of Moses. It seems apparent from his killing of the Egyptian in Exodus 2 that Moses had some sense that God had raised him up to be a deliverer for Israel. But he is trying to accomplish the will of God in his own way. When his act is discovered and Pharaoh tries to kill him, he flees into Midian, where he tends sheep for forty years. Now that he has lost all trust in himself and in his own ability to deliver the Israelites, God can use him. At the burning bush God resurrects the vision that had been dead those forty years, and through Moses accomplishes a mighty deliverance for His people. Not only do we see this pattern in the life of Moses and other Old Testament saints, but we can see it played out in our own lives as well.

FOR ME TO FOLLOW GOD

Every person has a purpose. God has created each of us to fill a unique role in His plan. Because God loves us, He invites us to join Him in His activity.

As Abraham followed God, God revealed His vision to Abraham step by step along the way. And obedience was costly, if only in Abraham's heart. Sometimes the cost was something Abraham had to give up, sometimes it was something he had to walk away from.

📖 At each of the following steps, what did Abraham's obedience cost him?

Genesis 12:1	
Genesis 14:21–23	
Genesis 17:18–19	
Genesis 21:9–12	
Genesis 22:2	

Obedience to God cost Abraham his homeland and family, the riches of a king, the covenant blessing for Ishmael as well as his presence in Abraham's life, and the life of Isaac.

Of all these things, what do you think was the hardest thing for Abraham to give up to God?

_____

Not only was Isaac Abraham's long-awaited son from his beloved wife Sarah, but he also embodied all the promises that God had given Abraham concerning his descendants and their land. In giving Isaac as a sacrifice to God, Abraham was trusting God completely with the vision.

 What are the things in your life in which you have to grit your teeth to trust God?

_____
_____
_____
_____

Why do you think God would want you to give those things to Him?

_____
_____
_____

> **God has created each of us to fill a unique role in His plan. Because God loves us, He invites us to join Him in His activity.**

> **In giving Isaac as a sacrifice to God, Abraham was trusting God completely with the vision.**

When we choose to let the vision die, He takes it and resurrects it, now purified from the stain of our ownership. God's vision for our life is always twofold: **1)** God's ultimate purpose in the world through me, and **2)** God's ultimate purpose in me. Through Abraham's life, God wanted to create a nation and a seed that would bless all the nations of the world. In Abraham's life, God wanted to grow a relationship with him characterized by faithful obedience and trust. God wants the same relationship with you, conforming you to the image of Christ (Romans 8:29).

Abraham learned that nothing in life compared with following God. We may not have an "Isaac" to lay on the altar, but every day we make choices that reveal where our heart is.

 How much control do you try to keep in each of the following areas? (Place an "X" in the appropriate location on the line.)

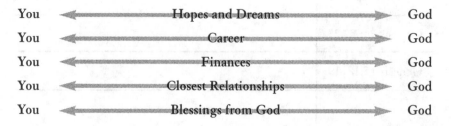

You	←	Hopes and Dreams	→	God
You	←	Career	→	God
You	←	Finances	→	God
You	←	Closest Relationships	→	God
You	←	Blessings from God	→	God

Now that you have a clearer view of the amount of control you are trying to hang on to, are you willing to release control of the vision so that God can do His work in and through you?

Where do you begin? With . . .

- ✓ **listening** to God's voice through consistent study of His word,
- ✓ **seeking** God and His way first in every area of your life through prayer, and
- ✓ **walking** daily in the realization that God is in control and that He is working all things together for your good.

Are you following God at any cost?

Spend some time in prayer with the Lord right now.

 Father, I want to know You, but my cowardly heart fears to give up its toys. I cannot part with them without inward bleeding, and I do not try to hide from You the terror of the parting. I come trembling, but I do come. Please root from my heart all those things which I have cherished so long and which have become a very part of my living self, so that You may enter and dwell there without a rival. Then you shall make the place of Your feet glorious. Then shall my heart have no need for the sun to shine in it, for You Yourself will be the light of it, and there will be no night there. In Jesus' name, Amen.

A. W. Tozer

Write out your prayer. Remind yourself that He is worth any cost He may request of you.

_____

_____

_____

_____

_____

_____

_____

_____

_____

_____

Notes

Choosing Not to Follow

*S*adly, the name of Lot, though designated in the New Testament as righteous, will ever be associated with the godless city of Sodom. His story is the tragic example of the miserable fall of a believer who fails to follow God. Lot is introduced in Scripture as the prospering nephew associated with his uncle, Abraham, *"the friend of God."* Yet his exit finds him living in a cave, having lost his wife, his sons and sons-in-law, and all of his wealth. All he has left in life is his two daughters, and his failure as a parent is reflected in the moral failure of his offspring, who get their father drunk and commit incest. Although Abraham was able to get Lot out of Sodom, he was not as successful in getting Sodom out of Lot. This week's lesson is not a pleasant one, but it serves as a faithful reminder of the disastrous consequences that occur when a child of God chooses not to follow Him.

Lot serves as a faithful reminder of the disastrous consequences that occur when a child of God chooses not to follow Him.

Where Does He Fit?

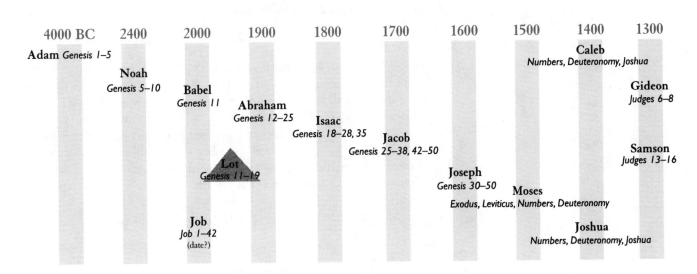

DAY ONE

STANDING IN THE SHADOWS OF GREATNESS

A man is not so much a product of his environment as he is of his choices.

From a cursory glance it would seem that providence placed Lot in the best possible place spiritually. He grew up in the shadow of the patriarch, Abraham. But from his life we see clearly that a man is not so much a product of his environment as he is a product of his choices. Consider the contrast between Lot and Abraham. Abraham grew up in the pagan land of the Chaldeans (modern-day Iraq), hardly an environment conducive to developing spirituality. He grew up surrounded by hedonistic people, yet he became the father of the faithful and through faith was reckoned righteous. (See Romans 4:12, 16.) Lot on the other hand grew up in the shadow of influence laid by Abraham, always within sight of a godly example as he followed God. Yet in this excellent environment for a growing faith, Lot chose to follow the world. Lot's life does not so much reflect his environment as it reflects his choices. Today we want to look closely at Lot's early life to see how he started his journey of faith.

📖 Read Genesis 11:27–28, 31. What was Lot's relationship to Abraham (Abram)?

_____

Who was apparently responsible for Lot after his father Haran's death?

_____

We see here that Lot is the son of Abram's brother, Haran. When Haran dies, Lot is cared for by his grandfather, Terah. The text gives us no idea of how old Lot was, but it is likely that he was a young adult, old enough to take on adult responsibilities, but evidently not yet married and still connected to his guardian, Terah.

📖 Read Genesis 11:31–32. Who all began the journey?

_____

Where were they headed?

_____

📖 Now read Acts 7:2–4. Who did God call to Canaan?

_____

Although the text suggests that it was Terah's idea to go to Canaan (in keeping with far-eastern custom and respect of the family patriarch), we see in Acts 7:2 that the call to Abraham first came while he was still in Ur. Most likely it was Abraham who persuaded his father to accompany him to the Promised Land. This idea is further supported by the fact that for undefined reasons the trip is halted at Haran (possibly, they established the city or at least were influential enough to see it named after Lot's deceased father). The journey begins again after Terah's death.

📖 Read Joshua 24:2–3. What do you learn about Terah's faith?

_____

_____

In Joshua 24, Joshua singles out Terah as an example of the way Israel's ancestors *"served other gods."* The implication of verse 3 is that there is a relationship between the idol worship of Terah and Abraham leaving Ur. It would seem that Abraham represented a turning point in this family line.

📖 Read Genesis 11:31—12:5. What happens in Haran (v. 32)?

_____

How would this have changed Lot's relationship with Abraham?

_____

After Terah dies, what does God direct Abraham to do (12:1)?

_____

_____

_____

Who does Abraham take with him (v. 5)?

_____

_____

_____

We see in Genesis 11:31 that Terah, as patriarch of the family clan is guardian to Lot. In verse 32 we are informed of Terah's death in Haran. Abraham is called by God to continue the journey and is given blessing and promise. We are told in Genesis 12:4 that when Abraham renews his journey to Canaan, Lot goes with him. Lot has gone from his father (Haran) to his grandfather (Terah) and now to his uncle, Abraham. In the Lord's providence a godly leader is now furnished, and following Abraham, Lot is once more on his way to the Promised Land.

Think about the tremendous opportunities God gave Lot by connecting him with Abraham. God had placed Lot in a great position to grow spiritually, but it was up to Lot to decide whether or not he would benefit.

🛑 **APPLY** What "Abrahams" has God placed in your life through whom you could be growing in Christ?

_____

_____

_____

God gives us opportunities, but He doesn't force us to take advantage of them. What do you need to change to keep from missing the blessings God has for you in those relationships?

_____

_____

_____

_____

God had placed Lot in a great position to grow spiritually, but it was up to Lot to decide whether or not he would benefit.

TROUBLE IN THE PROMISED LAND

We move forward in our journey, and years have passed. Abraham and Lot finally make it to the promised land of Canaan, but due to a famine in the land, they detour to Egypt. When Abraham and Lot finally travel back to Canaan from Egypt, Lot is a young man with livestock and wealth of his own. But all is not well in the family clan. Trouble has wedged its way into Lot's relationship with his uncle Abraham.

📖 Read Genesis 13:1–7. What caused the conflict between Abraham and Lot (vv. 5–7)?

_____

_____

_____

From where do you think Lot's wealth came?

_____

_____

Put Yourself In Their Shoes

ABRAHAM AND LOT

When Abraham recognized that he and Lot needed to separate, he gave Lot first choice of land, trusting God with whatever would be left. Are there any choices in your life where you have been striving to have your way instead of trusting God with the outcome?

After their time in Egypt, Abraham and Lot both return to the promised land wealthier men. Lot's wealth probably came from some sort of partnership with Abraham. Possibly, he was considered his uncle's heir at this point. At the least, he learned the "business" from Abraham. In those days, one of the main forms of wealth was livestock (cattle, sheep, goats, camels and donkeys). Because of their prosperity, their herds were so large there wasn't enough pasture to go around, so there began to be conflict between the two herds and those caring for them.

📖 Read Genesis 13:8–9. What solution does Abraham propose?

_____

_____

What does this says to you about his character?

_____

_____

_____

_____

Considering Abraham's age and position in the family, what choice did he have the right to make?

_____

_____

In essence, Abraham says, "My relationship with you is more important than these flocks. Let's not fight about it." He proposes that Lot choose the land he wants, and Abraham will take what is left. Notice Abraham says, *"Please let there be no strife between you and me . . . for we are brothers."* As the uncle and the elder, Abraham had more rights than Lot, but he deferred those rights and treated Lot as an equal. He even gives Lot first choice. He is making relationships the priority and he is taking the "low road" in the conflict.

📖 Now read Genesis 13:10–13. How does Lot respond?

_____

_____

_____

_____

What is motivating him to make this choice?

_____

_____

What do you think he should have done?

_____

_____

Lot's response is one of pure selfishness. He sees how good the valley looks and says, "I'll take all of that." The text reads accurately, _"So Lot chose for himself. . . ."_ What should he have done? He should have said, "No, Abraham, you choose first," but he took no thought for the one with the greater rights. Perhaps what most reflects Lot's values here is the fact that he chose the land because it looked good, and he didn't notice how exceedingly wicked the people of the land were. Lot's selfishness placed his possessions as more important than his relationship with Abraham, and they had to separate. Lot chose to serve his wealth rather than his relationship with Abraham and his need for spiritual guidance.

📖 Read Matthew 6:24. What does Christ say about divided loyalties?

_____

_____

_____

God blesses us with possessions and position, but any time those things get in the way of our relationship with God or others He has put in our lives, they are in the wrong place. Idols are the things in our lives that we consider before we consider God and His way; they are the things we serve. And when we are serving them, we are not serving God. Often, we may believe God has the priority in our lives, but the choices we make reveal otherwise.

APPLY What are the things in your life that you have put in a position of priority over your relationship with God?

_____

_____

_____

_____

_____

> ## "So Lot chose for himself. . . ."
> ## Genesis 13:11

TRUTH AND CONSEQUENCES

In fairness to Lot, we are looking at his story with hindsight—an advantage he did not have. We can see clearly what a terrible mistake he has made, but unfortunately he will not realize it until it is too late. He has picked Sodom, thinking he has acted shrewdly, but he has chosen foolishly indeed. Often God's greatest manifestation of judgment is giving us what we ask for so that He can teach us the foolishness of our ways. Today we want to focus on a divinely placed warning sign God put in Lot's path.

📖 Genesis 14:1–7 describes events of the previous twelve years in the valley of Sodom. What has been going on there?

_____

_____

_____

_____

We learn here that for twelve years the region of Sodom has been a conquered kingdom, subservient to other kings. In those days kings were representative not of countries but of cities. Each would have its own king. This alliance of four kings dominated the land Lot had chosen. Finally Sodom rebels, and for a year they experience freedom, but then the alliance returns to wage war.

📖 Read Genesis 14:8–12. What was the outcome of the resulting civil war in the valley?

_____

_____

_____

_____

The kings of the cities around Sodom take to arms and prepare for war, and it would seem they have the advantage, outnumbering the enemy five to four. The next thing we see is the kings running for their lives. The battle is a total loss. All their wealth is taken and along with it, Lot and his possessions.

📖 According to Genesis 14:12, why was Lot taken?

_____

_____

📖 Read Genesis 13:12 and Genesis 14:12. What do you find when you compare these verses?

_____

_____

Lot is taken because he is now living in Sodom. In chapter 13, he had *"moved his tents as far as Sodom,"* but now he has moved into the city. Lot has consistently chosen to associate himself more and more with the citizens of Sodom rather than with his Uncle Abraham. And that choice is costing him.

Appearances can be deceiving. From the mountaintop, the valley of Sodom looked like a treasure to Lot, but later it appeared to be more like a trap. Sinful choices always look good in the beginning.

📖 Read through Genesis 14:13–16. When Abraham hears of Lot's capture, how does he respond (v. 14)?

_____

_____

And what is the outcome of the battle (vv. 15–16)?

_____

_____

_____

As soon as Abraham learns of Lot's predicament, he and his allies run to the rescue. Though greatly outnumbered, God prospers Abraham's venture and he completely routs his nephew's captors. Not only does Abraham secure Lot's release, he also gets back all the spoils and the other people who had been taken captive. As he returns, Abraham meets Melchizedek and is reminded that it was God and not he who worked the deliverance (14:20).

One would think this brush with disaster would result in Lot taking a long, hard look at his life. He is indebted to Abraham and God even more for his life and wealth. Yet there is no indication that Lot has any change of heart, and apparently he goes back to living in the godless city of Sodom.

Just as Abraham rescued Lot from the consequences of his association with Sodom, God has rescued us from our sinful natures. But how often, just like Lot, do we say, "Thank you, Lord. I'm much obliged," and then turn around and walk right back into place, where we were in so much trouble to begin with. We set ourselves up for spiritual failure and act as if God's grace is cheap, a thing of little value.

 If this has been true of you recently, stop before you do anything else and confess it to the Lord. Ask Him to make real to you the true worthlessness of anything the world and your flesh has to offer. Ask Him to make it your fervent pursuit to daily follow God.

> **We set ourselves up for spiritual failure and act as if God's grace is cheap, a thing of little value.**

RESCUING THE RIGHTEOUS

Lot **DAY FOUR**

Moving ahead to Genesis chapter 18, we see that God reveals to Abraham the coming judgment of wicked Sodom. Certainly Abraham's compassion on that place is heightened by the knowledge that his nephew resides there. In a powerful illustration of intercession, we see Abraham asking God to spare the city because of the righteous who reside there. God promises to spare the city if there can be found only ten righteous residing there. Tragically not even ten righteous are discovered in this depraved area. Instead, God dispatches two angels to rescue Lot and his family. Today we want to see what we can learn from this sad episode in Lot's life.

📖 Read Genesis 19:1–11. Who does God send to Lot?

_____

And what happens that evening (vv. 4–5)?

_____

_____

How does Lot respond (vv. 6–8)?

_____

_____

How did the men of the city respond (v. 9)?

_____

_____

What happens next (vv. 10–11)?

_____

_____

_____

Two angels come to Sodom to where Lot is, and he invites them to stay with him. After dinner *all* the men of the city, young and old, come to Lot's house wanting to have homosexual relations with them. Lot tries to deter them, and they accuse him of judging them and threaten to rape him as well. In the end, the angels rescue Lot and strike the men with blindness. Even then, these wicked men are slow to give up their evil pursuit.

📖 Read Genesis 19:8, 12–16. Take this information, along with what you already know of Lot, and identify what you can about the people who made up his family.

_____

_____

Who ends up being rescued?

_____

We see in verse 8 that Lot has two virgin (unmarried) daughters. It is unclear if the "son-in-law" spoken of in verse 12 is one of the "sons-in-law" of verse 14 who are betrothed to his daughters or is already married to another daughter. We learn in verse 12 that he has "sons" (plural), and, of course, as revealed in verse 15, he has a wife. This is the first mention of Lot's wife, though their children are old enough to marry. It appears from what we have seen thus far that the wife is a Canaanite (probably a resident of Sodom). We learn from these verses that all the children were lost except for the two virgin daughters.

📖 Read Genesis 19:17 and 26. What did the angels command?

_____

_____

And what happened?

_____

_____

Lot lost all of his children save two daughters, and now he has lost his wife also. It's not hard to imagine why she looked back. Her home is being destroyed. Her children are dying. Probably, other friends and family were in the city. And so she looked back and died as well. Lot had chosen to settle and make a home in Sodom. He chose to marry a woman of Sodom, and it was only natural that her affections would be there. And he had to live with the consequences of those choices.

Lot chose to adjust his life to Sodom, though he apparently was recognized as having different values (19:9). Lot's personal behavior may have been righteous, but his life was entangled in Sodom. Not only were his riches there, but he had planted his affections in the city as well. And he lost almost everything.

📖 Read Genesis 19:17–29. Where do the angels want Lot to go?

_____

Where does Lot want to go (v. 20–22)?

_____

What difference do you think it makes for Lot at this point?

_____

_____

_____

Did You Know?
LOT'S WIFE

"*. . . and she became a pillar of salt.*" In *Antiquities 1, 2, 4,* Josephus wrote that this pillar still remained in his day and that he had seen it. It was a peculiar formation of crumbling, crystalline rock associated by tradition with the event in Genesis 19.

The two angels direct Lot to the mountains (toward Abraham), but Lot requests and is allowed to go to Zoar (toward Egypt). Apparently, if he can't stay in the cities, he at least wants to go to a town. Even in the end, Lot still wants to go his own way. One must question why, after all the kindness shown to him, Lot does not want to listen to God's direct guidance or flee to the care of Abraham.

📖 Now read Genesis 19:30–37, and summarize what occurs.

_____

_____

_____

_____

_____

_____

Lot does finally leave Zoar, but still he does not return to his kinsman, Abraham. At the end of his life we find this once wealthy man impoverished and living in a cave. His daughters are women of Sodom, and they get their father drunk and commit incest. Because Lot failed to walk in the ways of God, his daughters are a product of the city where they were born and raised. Lot continually chose his own way, and his daughters learned from him and from the environment in which he raised them. The wicked offspring of this ungodly union became the Moabites and Ammonites, countries that will war with Israel for centuries to come.

God would have spared Sodom if only ten righteous could have been found in that wicked place, but there were not ten righteous there. Looking at those who were spared, it would seem that Lot is the only one righteous. His two innocent daughters are spared, but their innocence does not last. Most of his own family perished in the judgment.

One wonders how Lot could even be called righteous, yet Peter uses this very word to describe him in 2 Peter 2:6–9. He states that in Sodom, because of what Lot saw and heard, he *"felt his righteous soul tormented day after day with their lawless deeds."* Lot was *"oppressed"* by the godless conduct of those unprincipled men, yet sadly, he was not offended enough by Sodom's wickedness to leave it behind. He has to be rescued. The biblical character of Lot tells the tragic tale of a believer snared in the mire of sin. There is no godly legacy in his family lineage. The same is true for every believer who lives for self instead of for God.

FOR ME TO FOLLOW GOD

In 2 Peter 2:6–9 we read,

> . . . *If* [God] *condemned the cities of Sodom and Gomorrah to destruction by reducing them to ashes, having made them an example to those who would live ungodly thereafter; and if He rescued righteous Lot, oppressed by the sensual conduct of unprincipled men (for by what he saw and heard that righteous man, while living among them, felt his righteous soul tormented day after day with their lawless deeds) then the Lord knows how to rescue the godly from temptation, and to keep the unrighteous under punishment for the day of judgment.*

Here we learn some significant things about Lot, and about God and our own relationship with Him as well.

📖 Read Genesis 18:20–21 and 19:13, 15, 24–25. How did God respond to the sin of Sodom and Gomorrah?

_____

_____

_____

God judged the inhabitants of these cities for their sin, and the sentence was destruction. God abhors sin, and He judges it. It's important for us to realize God's view of sin.

📖 Read the following verses, and write down what God says about sin.

Deuteronomy 9:3–5 _____

_____

Proverbs 15:9 _____

Isaiah 59:2 _____

Ephesians 5:5–6 _____

_____

James 4:17 _____

It's important for us to realize God's view of sin.

Sin is an abomination to a Holy God, and it requires His judgment. The Scripture is full of examples. Sin is our most basic and powerful problem. But God's justice does not supersede His mercy, and we also see that grace and mercy in God's dealings with Lot.

📖 Read Genesis 19:15–16. What do the angels do?

_____

Why were they so persistent (v. 16)?

_____

_____

"For the compassion of the LORD was upon him." Lot's poor choices, though they separated Lot from godly influences, did not alienate him from the Lord's compassion. God continually, both personally and through Abraham, intervened in Lot's life despite his foolish and selfish choices.

📖 Read the following verses, and write down what each says about the mercy and lovingkindness (compassion) of God.

Psalm 86:15 _____

_____

Isaiah 54:10 _____

_____

Lamentations 3:22–23 _____

_____

Luke 1:78–79 _____

_____

Romans 9:15–16 _____

_____

Ephesians 2:4–7 _____

_____

God's mercy and compassion are greater than we could ever comprehend, full and overflowing in our lives. Although Lot failed over and over in his choices, his relationship with God had not ended.

📖 Read 2 Peter 2:6–9. How is Lot depicted?

_____

_____

_____

Notice the ways he is described here: *"righteous Lot,"* having a *"righteous soul,"* as the *"godly"* being rescued. Even when we sin, God's mercy keeps the relationship going. But in the midst of God's mercy, Lot continued throughout his life to make foolish choices. He consistently chose what looked good in his eyes, and he lived with the consequences of those choices.

> ## "For the compassion of the LORD was upon him."
> ## Genesis 19:16

In hindsight, we can see Lot's poor choices clearly. But that is often true of our bad choices as well—we only recognize them in hindsight. So how can we avoid poor choices in our lives?

First, we need to recognize that God is God and we are not. That means that He knows what we are unable to know, and sees the poison of Sodom disguised in the lush beauty of the valley.

📖 Read Isaiah 46:9–10. What does God say He has declared?

_____

_____

God not only knows, but has purposed, all of time. It only makes sense to decide up front to go God's way. *"If the Lord is God, then follow Him!"* (1 Kings 18:21). When we are confronted with another way that looks reasonable and good, having already determined to choose God's way can make the decision far less confusing.

📖 According to 2 Peter 2:9, what does God know?

_____

_____

_____

"...the LORD knows how to rescue the godly from temptation, and to keep the unrighteous under punishment for the day of judgment."
2 Peter 2:9

God knows *"how to rescue the godly from temptation."* When we are following Him with our whole hearts, we are always moving safely away from temptation. We can trust Him. And if we are eager to follow God, then we will be seeking His direction in prayer.

📖 Read 1 John 5:14–15. What confidence do we have in God?

_____

_____

God's will in our lives is not some mysterious point we'll get to eventually. It's how He wants us to walk every day. He's not trying to hide it. Too often, we're just not willing to see it because we're too busy trying to convince ourselves that what we want really is God's will. Our Father wants us to ask Him what to do and obey what He says every day.

God has given us His guiding principles for our lives in His Word. We can tell God we want His will in our lives, but our actions prove our words a lie when we don't bother to study what He has revealed to us in His Word.

📖 Read James 1:22–25. What instructions are we given concerning God's Word?

_____

_____

What is the result for the man who obeys (v. 25)?

_____

We are to *do* what the Word tells us to do, and not delude ourselves into believing we are spiritual just because of the Bible knowledge we may possess.

Lot was given the benefit of Abraham's example and intervention in his life, as well as the instructions of God. But it was not an asset in his life because he did not act on it; instead, he insisted on his own way—what looked good to him.

Lot's decisions are a warning to all of us not to choose our own way, and not to try to compromise God's will with our own. Lot did seek God (God refers to him as *"righteous"*), but he also sought his own self-interests. God's judgment on Lot was simply allowing him to have what he wanted—Sodom. And in the end, he lost the very things he had selfishly worked to gain.

So how do we avoid foolish choices? By seeking the wise ones.

1. Accept that God is God and you're not. In His wisdom, He knows the way for you to go.

2. Pray daily, asking Him to guide you in His will throughout the day.

3. Seek His guidance through Bible study. He gave us His Word to reveal to us Himself and His will for our lives.

Spend some time with the Lord in prayer.

 Lord, forgive me for my selfishness and thank You for so often protecting me from my own foolishness. I choose to follow You; help me to see the lie of all the world has to offer. Show me what I am, Lord, and teach me the true value of Your grace. I would not take it for granted. Please rid my heart of all selfish ambition, and make my only ambition be to follow You each day with all that I am. In Jesus' name, Amen.

Write out your own prayer to the Lord, Who wants to lovingly guide you all your life.

_____

_____

_____

_____

_____

_____

_____

_____

_____

_____

> ## Lot's decisions are a warning to all of us not to choose our own way.

Notes

Jacob

FOLLOWING GOD IN LIFE'S JOURNEYS

*J*acob's journeys are some of the most intriguing life journeys in all of Scripture. Jacob's life is noteworthy from the start—even before he was born his struggles with his twin Esau were the subject of a special revelation to his mother Rebekah concerning the destiny of both boys and the nations who would descend from them.

Jacob experienced seven revelations from the Lord in his journeys, and in those revelations we discover Jacob learning to follow God—to hear His word and obey. Those revelations occurred around five significant turning points in Jacob's life, turning points designed by God to fulfill the destiny He had for Jacob. But these turning points were also part of God's destiny for His people Israel, for His Son the Messiah, and for all His redeemed throughout the ages—all those who have been, are now, or ever will be on the journey of following God.

In Jacob's journey of following God we can see a lifetime of highs and lows, failures and successes. We see clearly that following God is a process of learning to hear God's Word and obey.

WHERE DOES HE FIT?

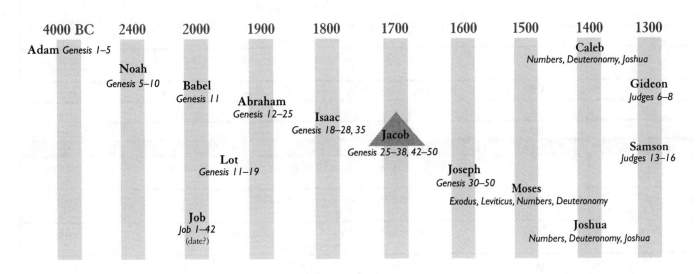

4000 BC	2400	2000	1900	1800	1700	1600	1500	1400	1300

Adam *Genesis 1–5*

Noah
Genesis 5–10

Babel
Genesis 11

Abraham
Genesis 12–25

Isaac
Genesis 18–28, 35

Jacob
Genesis 25–38, 42–50

Lot
Genesis 11–19

Joseph
Genesis 30–50

Moses
Exodus, Leviticus, Numbers, Deuteronomy

Caleb
Numbers, Deuteronomy, Joshua

Gideon
Judges 6–8

Samson
Judges 13–16

Joshua
Numbers, Deuteronomy, Joshua

Job
Job 1–42
(date?)

A Look at Jacob's Life

Genesis	Jacob's Age	Events	Place
25:21–26	Infant	Jacob struggles with Esau in the womb and after his birth.	Living in Negev (Gen. 24:62)
25:27–34	40 or younger	Jacob steals birthright from Esau.	Negev
		Esau marries at age forty (26:34).	Beersheba
27:1–46	77	Jacob deceives Isaac into giving him the Blessing.	Beersheba
FIRST TURNING POINT			
28:1–22	77	Jacob flees Esau's anger. Jacob dreams of the Ladder or Staircase to Heaven, in which he receives the promise of Land, Nation, Seed.	Bethel
29:1–15	77	Jacob meets Rachel and Laban.	Haran (Paddan-aram, modern Syria)
29:16–20	77–84	Jacob works for Laban for Rachel's hand in marriage.	Haran
29:20–35 30:1–24	84–91	Jacob marries Leah and Rachel at age 84, works seven more years for Laban, and begins having children	Haran
30:25–43	91–97	Jacob agrees to work for Laban for livestock	Haran
SECOND TURNING POINT			
31	97	God calls Jacob to return to Canaan.	
31:1–55	97	Jacob flees from Laban. Covenant of the Mizpah with Laban	Hill country of Gilead
32:1–22	97	Jacob prepares to meet Esau.	
THIRD TURNING POINT			
32:1–32	97	Jacob wrestles with the Angel of the Lord.	River Jabbok
33:1–17	97	Jacob meets Esau after twenty years.	
33:18–20	97	Jacob settles in Shechem.	
33:18–20 34:1–31	97–107	Dinah is defiled in Shechem. Men of Shechem are slain.	Shechem
FOURTH TURNING POINT			
35:1–15	107	God calls Jacob back to Bethel.	
35:1–15	107	Jacob moves to Bethel. (Name is changed to Israel.)	Bethel
35:16–27	108	On a journey to Ephrath (near Bethlehem), Rachel gives birth to Benjamin and dies. Jacob settles in Hebron.	Near Bethlehem Hebron
37:1–36	108	Joseph's brothers hate him and sell him into slavery. Joseph is taken to Egypt.	Dwelling in valley of Hebron, Shechem, Dothan
38:1–30		Incident of Judah and Canaanite woman and of Judah and Tamar	Chezib, Timnah and the area around there
35:28–29	120	Isaac dies in Hebron.	Hebron
39—41	108–129	Joseph in Egypt—slave, in prison, exalted, famine begins	Egypt Canaan
42:1–38	129	Jacob's ten sons go to Egypt to buy grain. Simeon is held prisoner.	Egypt
43–45	129	Sons return to Egypt for grain. Joseph reveals himself as their brother.	Egypt
45:21–28	129	Brothers return to Jacob with news of Joseph.	Canaan
FIFTH TURNING POINT			
46:1–4	130	Jacob offers sacrifices, and God speaks to Jacob at Beersheba.	Beersheba en route to Egypt
46:5–34 47:1–31	130–147	Jacob and family settle into the land of Goshen in Egypt.	Goshen in Egypt
48—49	147	Jacob's last days, blessings on Ephraim and Manasseh, prophecies concerning his 12 sons	Egypt
49:29–33	147	Death of Jacob (Israel), burial at Machpelah with Abraham, Sarah, Isaac, Rebekah, and Leah	Egypt Machpelah

JACOB STARTS HIS JOURNEYS

The birth of Jacob and his brother Esau came in answer to prayer. After twenty years of marriage, Isaac and Rebekah still had no children. Genesis 25:21–22 says Isaac prayed for his barren wife and *"the LORD answered him."* As she carried this gift of God, *"the children struggled together within her."* The Lord revealed that two nations would come from her womb, and the older would serve the younger. Implied in this was the struggle that the Scriptures will unfold.

📖 In the chart below, list the differences you see between Esau and Jacob in Genesis 25:23–28.

Jacob	Esau

The appearance of Esau and Jacob was certainly different. In addition, Esau, the older, was a skillful hunter and a man of the field. Isaac, who had a taste for game, had a deep love for Esau. Jacob, the younger, named the supplanter, the "heel-grabber," was a peaceful man who stayed in the tents. Rebekah favored him.

Another contrast between Jacob and Esau can be seen in their attitudes toward the birthright. The birthright, in the case of the sons of Isaac, meant being part of the promises made to Abraham and Isaac which included a land, a nation, and a seed. That meant being in the line of the Messiah to come.

📖 Read Genesis 25:29–34. What do you find out about Jacob's attitude toward the birthright?

_____

_____

_____

_____

_____

What about Esau's attitude?

_____

_____

_____

_____

_____

Put Yourself In Their Shoes

THE FIRSTBORN AND THE BIRTHRIGHT

As his birthright, the firstborn:

• received a double portion of the inheritance;

• became head of the family upon the father's death;

• served as the spiritual leader/priest of the family;

• was given great authority and honor.

As the story progresses it becomes evident that Jacob thought of the birthright as a valued prize worth gaining, and he used his cunning to obtain it. For Esau it was worth no more than a bowl of stew—no more than a passing physical desire. Genesis 25:34 says he *"despised his birthright,"* indicating that the hunger incident did not make him despise it. It simply brought to light the attitude that was already in his heart.

Approximately 37 years later Isaac, at age 137 thinking of the possibility of his death, desired to bestow his blessing on Esau. Rebekah overheard their conversation and wanted that blessing for Jacob. The blessing of Isaac on Jacob would match the prophecy the Lord had given Rebekah before the birth of the boys—the older would serve the younger and experience greater blessing and strength.

Read Genesis 27:1–29. What was the plan that Rebekah devised?

_____

_____

_____

Knowing what God had prophesied for her sons (Genesis 25:22–23), why would Rebekah have done this?

_____

_____

_____

How did Jacob respond when his mother proposed the plan?

_____

_____

_____

How did he respond to Isaac's question in verse 20?

_____

_____

_____

Jacob and Rebekah sought by deceit what God had promised and wanted to give by His design.

What does this tell you about his character?

_____

_____

_____

In verses 30–46, what resulted from Jacob's deception?

_____

_____

_____

It is evident that Rebekah initiated this plot to steal the blessing, and that Jacob wanted the blessing even at the expense of lying and deceiving his father. Esau saw this as another deceitful trick of Jacob—first the birthright and now the blessing. As a result he wanted to kill his brother and planned to do so. Rebekah saw the dangers ahead and arranged for Jacob to flee to Haran to her brother Laban for *"a few days."* On his journey to Laban's home, he came to a place called Luz. This was the **first turning point** in Jacob's life.

Read Genesis 28:10–22. Was Jacob looking for God in his journey?

_____

List nine things God told Jacob.

_____

_____

_____

_____

_____

_____

_____

_____

Jacob was not looking for the Lord. The Lord came to him in a dream and revealed Himself as the covenant God of Abraham and Isaac—the God about whom he had heard so much. The Lord promised Jacob the land of Canaan, many descendants (a nation), and a seed in whom all the families of the earth would be blessed. In addition God promised . . .

- His presence (*"I will be with you."*)
- His protection (*"I will keep you wherever you go."*)
- His promise of return (*"I will bring you back to this land."*)
- His providential guarantee (*"I will not leave you until I have done what I have promised you."*)

When he woke up, what was Jacob's response?

_____

_____

_____

_____

Word Study

BETHEL

The Hebrew is *Beyth-El*, from the words *bayith*, meaning "house," and *el*, meaning "the Almighty, God." Thus Jacob renamed Luz, "the House of God."

Jacob responded with a vow declaring that the Lord would be his God, this place would be called *"Bethel,"* and he would give a tenth of all he had to God. Jacob's life was now marked by a new commitment. His life would never be the same.

HARAN BECOMES HOME

Jacob's journey took him 440 miles from Beersheba to the city of Haran and the home of Laban, Rebekah's brother. There he met the family and became engaged to Rachel. He agreed to work for Laban seven years that he might marry her. His days of labor *"seemed to him but a few days because of his love for her"* (Genesis 29:20). When the wedding day came he discovered two things: first, Laban was even more deceitful than he was, and second, he was married to Leah, Rachel's older sister. Laban informed him that this was the custom. Rachel could also be his wife, but it would mean seven more years of working for Laban. Jacob agreed to that. Over the next seven years, eleven sons and a daughter were born to Jacob (29:31–35; 30:1–24). After fourteen years with Laban, Jacob was ready to take his family and go back to Canaan. Laban convinced him to work a few more years for pay in livestock.

Both men agreed Laban's livestock did well under Jacob's care. Jacob bargained for the speckled, spotted, and black livestock. His livestock multiplied, and in six years time he was *"exceedingly prosperous"* (Genesis 30:43). But this was also a difficult time for Jacob. Laban changed his wages ten times and appears to have been deceitful and underhanded in some of his dealings. Jacob was ready to leave.

📖 Genesis 31:1–16 records the **second turning point** in Jacob's life. Who initiated this turning point? (Note: see v. 12 for a glimpse of God's heart towards Jacob.)

_____

_____

In verses 14–16, what was Leah's and Rebekah's response to the proposed move?

_____

_____

_____

What did God use to prepare their hearts to leave their home?

_____

_____

_____

_____

Did You Know?
LABAN'S HOUSEHOLD IDOLS

In Genesis 31, Laban pursues Jacob and his family because his household gods have been stolen. Rachel succeeds in hiding the idols from her father.

Possession of these household gods probably implied leadership of the family, and in the case of a married daughter, made her husband rightful heir to her father's property. in Genesis 31, Rachel is apparently trying to secure the right of inheritance to Laban's property for Jacob.

According to Genesis 31:1–2, the attitude of Laban and his sons grew less and less friendly. In the midst of this, the Lord spoke and told Jacob to return to his first home—to the land of his father and relatives. He promised His presence. God clearly initiated this move back to Canaan. When Jacob talked to his wives, he reminded them of the ways of Laban and the faithfulness of God through it all, including the transfer of abundant livestock to Jacob. Then, Jacob recounted a dream God had given him confirming these truths of Laban's ways and God's care, protection, and provision. Rachel and Leah agreed. Their answer serves as a model for anyone seeking to follow God: *"now then, do whatever God has said to you"* (v. 16). Jacob's move back to Canaan, however, would not be complete until he dealt with the issue of Esau.

📖 Read Jacob's prayer in Genesis 32:9–12. To what is Jacob appealing? (Check all that apply)

☐ God's original promise	☐ His own unworthiness
☐ Jacob's rights—he earned it.	☐ His ability to protect his own
☐ Esau's forgiveness	☐ God's promise to prosper him
☐ God's faithfulness	☐ God's deliverance
☐ God's promise to his descendants	☐ His own fear

Jacob had first sent messengers to Esau, hoping to find favor in his sight. When he heard Esau was coming with four hundred men Jacob became *"greatly afraid and distressed."* He divided those with him into two companies and then went to the Lord in prayer, recounting the Lord's faithfulness and the Lord's promises to him and asking Him to fulfill His promises of protection. Then he arranged gifts to be sent ahead to Esau—three droves of livestock (over 550 head of livestock, an indication of the great prosperity God had given him). He then sent his family across the Jabbok, and he was left alone. All alone Jacob had another encounter with the Lord. This was the **third turning point** in his life.

📖 Read Genesis 32:24–32. When *"a man"* grabbed Jacob and wrestled with him, with whom do you suppose Jacob thought he was wrestling?

_____

_____

Initially, Jacob probably thought it was Esau or one of his men, since that was his biggest fear at the time. Or perhaps he thought Laban had renewed their rivalry. Or maybe it was a robber. In any case, the last thing Jacob expected was to find himself wrestling with God. Often in life, we think our struggle is with another person or a situation, when ultimately, it is with God.

📖 Look at 32:24–25. At daybreak, when Jacob is still wrestling with God, what does God do?

_____

_____

_____

Why do you think God was unable to prevail against Jacob?

_____

_____

_____

Often in life, we think our struggle is with another person or a situation, when ultimately, it is with God.

The Hebrew word here for *"prevailed"* (*yakol*) means "to overcome." It was not that God wasn't strong enough to defeat Jacob physically, for all God had to do was *"touch"* Jacob's hip and it dislocated. It wasn't that God was unable to overpower Jacob's body; it was that He couldn't overcome his *will*. Jacob was too stubborn to "say uncle," so God had to raise the stakes by causing him pain.

Sometimes we cause ourselves unnecessary pain because of our unwillingness to surrender. God, in His mercy and grace, is willing to allow us to experience pain in order to bring us to the point of surrender to Him and to His ways. When Jacob realized that, due to his injury, he could not win, he chose to surrender the contest but to hold on to God and seek His blessing. He realized that this was no ordinary man, no ordinary contest, no ordinary prize.

 Can you recall a time in your life when God "crippled" you (made you weak) to bring you to a point of surrender—where you would embrace Him and His ways instead of your own?

_____

_____

_____

_____

Jacob finally embraced God because he knew he could trust Him. He had seen the trustworthiness of God through the past twenty years in Haran. It had not been a time without difficulties, but in the midst of those difficulties, God was faithful to the promises He had made at Bethel. Jacob's hope remained in God. The promises God gave Jacob at Bethel are the same promises God has given us in Christ: His presence (Hebrews 13:5), His protection (2 Timothy 4:18), and His provision (John 10:10; 14:1–3). Our hope is sure.

Jacob had just come from his encounter with Laban. That was behind him. Now he faced an encounter with Esau, but God had another encounter in mind. Jacob must face God, and he must face himself and his ways. And he must fight to the point of surrender. A Man met him that night. According to Hosea 12:3–4, it was the Angel of the Lord (who most theologians recognize as the pre-incarnate Christ) who began the wrestling match that would forever mark Jacob. This was a contest in which tripping someone was a skill. But Jacob found he could not win. Then, the Man touched him and disabled him at the strongest point in a wrestler's leg.

The wrestling match was an illustration of Jacob's life to that point—fighting and deceiving to get for himself. But now he was crippled, helpless against this Man and against the approaching Esau. He would have to depend on the Lord, so he cried out in prayer with tears for His blessing (Hosea 12:3–4). At that point his name was changed to Israel—_"he who strives with God."_ The one who wants God's way and fights to get it. The one who strives with God and surrenders to Him and His way knows the blessings of God and His answers to prayer.

God wants us to want what He wants for us. Often we have to wrestle to that point of surrender, but that is the point of blessing.

Jacob did receive the blessing of the Lord. He was learning that God wants us to want what He wants for us. Often we have to wrestle to that point of surrender, but that is the point of blessing. This was the most crucial turning point in Jacob's life—he was changed on the inside. The victories and assurances only God can give became his. If Israel would prevail now, it would be by the blessing and the hand of God not by the cunning and strength of Jacob.

In the morning Jacob limped out to meet Esau. The two brothers embraced and wept, and then parted at peace with one another (Genesis 33:4–17).

Jacob moved to Succoth, then Shechem. In Shechem Jacob learned the tragic lesson of what happens when the covenant people of God mix with the ungodly influences of Canaan. Genesis 34 recounts the story of Jacob's daughter, Dinah, mixing with the women of the land and being attacked as a result. Simeon and Levi take revenge, and there is a bloody massacre of the Canaanite men. That became the setting for another encounter with the Lord and the **fourth turning point** in Jacob's life.

THE FOURTH TURNING POINT: BACK TO BETHEL

Jacob had lived in Canaan, in the city of Shechem, almost ten years and had allowed idols to become a part of his household. He also had not fulfilled his vow (at Bethel) to honor God as his God and give a tenth of all to Him. Now, Jacob was deeply concerned that the circumstances in Shechem would spell disaster for him and his family. At that point the Lord spoke to Jacob giving him clear direction.

📖 Read Genesis 35:1–7.

What were the Lord's specific directions?	What did Jacob do in response?
1. _____	_____
_____	_____
2. _____	_____
_____	_____
3. _____	_____
_____	_____

In Jacob's distress, God brought him back to Bethel— back to His design for his life.

The Lord told Jacob to leave Shechem, go to Bethel (15 miles south), and live there. He was to make an altar there to God—the God who appeared to him at Bethel thirty years before when he was fleeing from Esau. Jacob responded with prompt obedience. He called his family to **1)** put away all the foreign gods, **2)** purify themselves, and **3)** in light of these changes, change garments. They would all go to Bethel to worship the true Lord there at the altar Jacob would build. Jacob knew he could not follow God and stay where he was.

📖 In verse 5, why did a *"great terror"* come upon the cities by which they passed?

_____

_____

_____

According to verse 3, on what did Jacob rely for protection?

_____

_____

In line with Jacob's testimony about the Lord being with him *"wherever I have gone,"* they experienced the protection of the Lord with them on their journey. At Bethel, the place of obedient worship, the Lord appeared to Jacob once again.

📖 Read Genesis 35:9–15. God uses the name God Almighty, or El Shaddai, which refers to the abundant fruitfulness and strength God has and gives. List the things of which God reminds Jacob in this meeting.

_____

_____

_____

_____

What did Jacob do in response?

_____

_____

Why would God specifically use His name "El Shaddai" in this context?

_____

_____

_____

God Almighty (El Shaddai), the giver of abundant fruitfulness and nourishment, promised Jacob the fruitfulness only He could give.

The Lord blessed Jacob and confirmed his new name Israel, the name that would be associated with the fulfillment of the covenant blessings through God's power. God revealed Himself as God Almighty (El Shaddai), the giver of abundant fruitfulness and nourishment. Based on who He is, He promised fruitfulness for Jacob, which included a nation and a land. There Jacob set up a pillar and worshiped. The pillar stood as a reminder that the Lord would indeed fulfill His will for His people and through them bring blessing to the world.

After this, Jacob journeyed south. On the way Rachel died near Bethlehem giving birth to Jacob's twelfth son, Benjamin. The family of Israel was complete. Jacob, at age 108, settled near Isaac in Hebron.

Jacob DAY FOUR

THE LONG JOURNEY TO EGYPT

In the year they moved to Hebron, the **final turning point** began for Jacob and his family. It would take twenty–three years to complete. Jacob, because of his deep love for Joseph (Rachel's oldest son) gave him a multi-colored tunic which symbolized his favor and most likely set him apart with the honors of the firstborn (37:3). This would have occurred soon after Reuben forfeited those rights through his incest with Bilhah, Jacob's concubine (35:22). The brothers of Joseph resented this favored position given by their father. They hated Joseph. After Joseph told them of his dreams indicating they would bow to him, they hated him even more. When the opportunity came, they sold him into slavery to Midianite traders. The traders sold him in Egypt to Potiphar, the captain of Pharaoh's bodyguard.

But what his brothers meant for evil against Joseph, God meant for good. Years later, Joseph had become second only to the Pharaoh in power, and is in a position to help his family when famine strikes the land. His brothers came to Egypt to buy food. Joseph, confronted with his brothers who do not recognize him, tested them to see if they have changed. Could they be trusted? He asked them to bring their youngest brother to Egypt to prove they were honest men and not spies. He kept Simeon prisoner until they returned. When the brothers arrived back in Canaan, they related all that had happened to their father. This was an intense trial for Jacob.

📖 Read Genesis 42:29–38 and 43:1–15. What was Jacob's attitude towards the situation (vv. 36, 6, 14)?

_____

_____

_____

_____

What response do you see from the brothers to the situation (vv. 37, 7–9)?

_____

_____

_____

_____

Jacob thought *"all these things are against me"* and refused to send Benjamin, believing that if he lost his youngest son too, it would bring him to his death through grief. Reuben offered his two sons as a guarantee of Benjamin's safety, and Judah later offered himself. Finally, pressed by the famine, Jacob agreed to send Benjamin to Egypt with his brothers.

When the brothers arrived in Egypt, Joseph was overcome at seeing Benjamin. He revealed himself and sent them back to bring Jacob (now called Israel) and all his family to Egypt. However, Jacob was living in Hebron, in the land of God's promise, the land God had given for him and his descendants. And now he learned that Joseph was alive and prospering in Egypt. His sons had returned with the wagons and provisions Joseph sent to bring them all back to Egypt. Jacob's anticipation of seeing Joseph again must have been overwhelming. All the circumstances were pointing towards Egypt, and Jacob began the journey, stopping at Beersheba to offer sacrifices to God. This was the setting for the **final turning point** in Jacob's life. There at Beersheba God spoke to him.

Did You Know?

BEERSHEBA

Beersheba was where Isaac's household had been when Esau sold his birthright to Jacob for a bowl of stew. Jacob had come a long way from the schemer he was then to the man who eventually learned to God.

📖 Read Genesis 46:1–5. In verse 3, God tells Jacob not to be afraid to go to Egypt. What are some of the things you think might have made Jacob afraid?

_____

_____

_____

_____

_____

The circumstances around him and his longing to see Joseph were sweeping Jacob along towards Egypt. But God's promises were in Canaan. And Jacob wanted God's promises.

In verses 3 and 4, what are the things of which God assured Jacob?

_____

_____

_____

_____

In Jacob's limited understanding and perspective, God met him at Beersheba, comforted his fears, and gave him the assurance that Egypt was part of His plan. God spoke to him and assured him of who He was as God, that he had no need to fear going to Egypt, and that He would make him a great nation there. He told him His presence would go with him to Egypt and that He would bring him up again. He would surely see Joseph, and Joseph would be the one to close his eyes in death. With that Jacob traveled to Egypt comforted and confident in the Lord's direction for him.

Jacob, at the age of 130, rejoiced greatly to see his son Joseph in Egypt. He would live there seventeen years and see his family receive outstanding care. There he blessed the sons of Joseph, Ephraim and Manasseh, and he prophesied over his twelve sons. Hebrews 11:21 reveals the heart of Jacob in this way: _"By faith Jacob, as he was dying, blessed each of the sons of Joseph, and worshiped, leaning on the top of his staff."_

📖 Read Jacob's blessing of Joseph in Genesis 48:15–16. Now that Jacob is dying, what is his perspective of his relationship with God through the journeys of his life?

_____

_____

_____

APPLY As you look at your life, how do you see God's mercy and grace working in you and your circumstances in spite of yourself?

_____

_____

_____

Jacob saw himself alligned with his fathers, Abraham and Isaac. They followed God, and he did as well. He saw God as his Shepherd *"all my life to this day"* and acknowledged that the angel of the Lord had *"redeemed me from all evil."* He knew God had cared for him, had led him through many difficult days, and had sustained him and blessed him through many turns in the journey.

After Jacob blessed his twelve sons he gave instructions for his burial in the cave of Machpelah at Hebron with Abraham, Sarah, Isaac, Rebekah, and Leah. Then he *"breathed his last, and was gathered to his people."* It was the end of a journey of 147 years with many tears and many joys, hundreds of miles guided by the Shepherd of Israel, and a sure knowledge of the blessing of following the covenant-keeping God of Abraham, Isaac, and Jacob.

FOR ME TO FOLLOW GOD

Jacob DAY FIVE

Fill in the following table according to each question:

	Genesis 27:6–20	Genesis 32:24–30	Genesis 35:1–7	Genesis 48:15–16
In a few words, describe Jacob's character according to each passage.				
In a few words, describe God's character according to each passage.				

What differences do you see in Jacob's character between Genesis 27 and Genesis 48?

_____

_____

_____

Do you see the same progression in God's character? _____

What does this tell you about God's relationship with us?

_____

_____

_____

No matter how Jacob responded to the circumstances in his life, God was always faithful, unchanging, and true to His promises.

Throughout his life, Jacob journeyed through times of doubt and fear, hardship and danger, peace and trust. He learned surrender and faithfulness to God. But no matter how Jacob responded to the circumstances in his life, God was always faithful, unchanging, and true to His promises.

APPLY Describe the spiritual journey in your own life:

What were you like before you met Christ?

_____

_____

_____

_____

Describe 3 or 4 milestones in your spiritual journey since you met Christ.

_____

_____

_____

_____

_____

In Genesis 48:15–16, at the end of his life, Jacob realized two things: **1)** that God had been his Shepherd all of his life, and **2)** that God had redeemed him *"from all evil."*

APPLY Is there some evil in your life that you need to address with God? Is there someone or something you are allowing to lead you into deception (Genesis 27:6–20)?

_____

_____

_____

Are you striving **against** God in any area of your life (Genesis 32:24–30)?

_____

_____

_____

What idols in your life do you need to take out and bury so that you can worship God (Genesis 35:1–7)?

_____

_____

_____

When we recognize our weakness and yield to God's strength, then we receive His blessings and learn daily to follow Him.

As we choose to forsake our flesh, God enables us to walk faithfully in accordance with that choice as we remain yielded to His control. Jacob never reached perfection here on earth, but there was a clear pattern of progression in his spiritual journey. When we recognize our weakness and yield to His strength, then we receive His blessings and daily learn to follow Him.

Spend some time in prayer to the Lord right now.

 Lord, how excellent are Your ways, and how devious and dark are the ways of man. Show me how to die, that I may rise again to newness of life. I have heard Your Word inviting me to look away to You and be satisfied. My heart longs to respond, but sin has clouded my vision till I see You but dimly. Be pleased to cleanse me in Your own precious blood, and make me inwardly pure, so that I may gaze upon You with unveiled eyes all the days of my earthly journey. By Christ's mercy, Amen.

A. W. Tozer

Write out your prayer. Thank Him for His faithfulness even in your failures.

_____

_____

_____

_____

_____

_____

_____

_____

_____

_____

"O Lord, our Lord, how excellent is Thy name in all the earth."

Psalm 8:9

Notes

FOLLOWING GOD WHEN THE PRESSURE'S ON

What an incredible life story! When we turn to the life of Joseph in Genesis, we encounter one of the most unique men in all of Scripture. Joseph faced a multitude of pressures and trials, any one of which could have caused him to give up hope, give in to the pressure, or turn away from God. He could have accused God of being powerless to handle his difficulties or, even worse, not caring enough to come and rescue him out of them. But Joseph did none of these. Instead, he knew some things about God. He trusted in God and what he had been told and taught about Him. And he had discovered the rich treasure of fearing God and walking in His presence. That is what we want to discover, and Joseph will help us.

Joseph discovered the rich treasure of fearing God and walking in His ways.

WHERE DOES HE FIT?

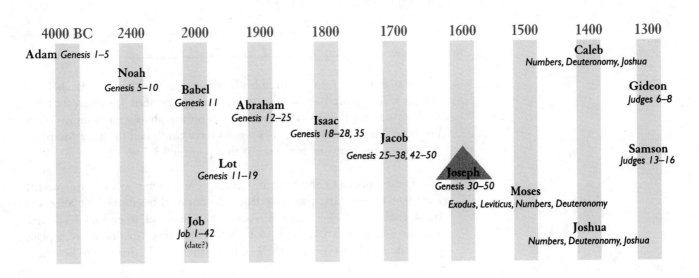

GROWING UP HAS ITS PRESSURES

Joseph was the eleventh of twelve sons born to Jacob through his two wives, Leah and Rachel, and their handmaidens, Zilpah and Bilhah. Joseph was Rachel's first-born son. He was the grandson of Isaac and the great grandson of Abraham. What was this family like into which he was born? What kind of pressures did he face growing up?

Genesis 29:21–35 tells us about Joseph's family. His father Jacob was tricked into taking Leah as his first wife and then was given Rachel as a second wife. At first, Leah bore four sons to Jacob, but it was evident that she was unloved and second-rate in his mind (v. 31). Though Jacob loved Rachel deeply, she bore him no children (vv. 30–31). Relationships between Rachel and Zilpah and Bilhah became strained, and this conflict affected the children as they grew.

In Genesis 30:1–24 we see many pressures recorded. In jealousy, both Rachel and Leah offered their maids to bear children to Jacob in their own names, and the result was ten sons by three different mothers. The Lord then finally opened Rachel's womb, and she bore Jacob an eleventh son named Joseph. The favored wife had given Jacob a son after some seven years of barrenness. When Joseph was born, his ten brothers ranged in age from one or two years old to six or seven years old. The four oldest boys were sons of Leah and were beginning to notice the differences between the relationship Jacob had with their mother and his relationship with Rachel.

Six years after Joseph was born, Jacob finally left his father-in-law's home. After an adventurous journey, Jacob and his family arrived in his homeland of Canaan and settled there. During these journeys and over the next ten years (approximately age seven to seventeen) Joseph grew into a young man. He learned much from the instruction and example of his father Jacob.

📖 Read Genesis 33:1–2. How is Joseph treated?

_____

_____

What do you think this tells Joseph? (Remember, Joseph is about seven years old at this time.)

_____

_____

The way in which Jacob secured his family made it evident that Rachel and Joseph were favored above all the rest—more protected, more cared for. This status doubtless made an impression on Joseph as well as on his older brothers. These family dynamics would have continued to shape Joseph in more ways than anyone could see at that point in his life.

The family moved to Shechem and lived there for ten years. Once again the family faced pressure, this time from the enraged inhabitants of Shechem (see Genesis 34). Genesis 35:1–3 records the Lord's call to go back to Bethel. He instructed Jacob to move back to Bethel and make an altar there, a place of worship and surrender to the Lord. In other words, this was to be a time

Did You Know?

THE SONS OF JACOB

1. Reuben (Leah)
2. Simeon (Leah)
3. Levi (Leah)
4. Judah (Leah)
5. Dan (Bilhah)
6. Naphtali (Bilhah)
7. Gad (Zilpah)
8. Asher (Zilpah)
9. Issachar (Leah)
10. Zebulun (Leah)
11. **Joseph** (Rachel)
12. Benjamin (Rachel)

of fresh surrender as well as a new start in a new place, all part of the journey God had for Jacob and his family. Joseph was an impressionable young man around the age of sixteen or seventeen. He would have seen Jacob leading his household to focus on the one true God and to put away any foreign gods. It was a time of cleansing from anything displeasing to the Lord. Jacob testified about the reality of God in his life—the faithfulness of God in every place he had been, and in all situations and times. And this, too, would have made an impression on Joseph.

📖 Read Genesis 35:9–15, looking at the encounter through Joseph's eyes. How do you think Joseph viewed the covenant promises made to his father Jacob at Bethel?

_____

_____

_____

_____

God affirmed Jacob's new name, Israel, at Bethel. This was a time of confirmation of the covenant with Jacob, just as the Lord had done with Abraham and Isaac. He was promised a nation, kings, and a land. Joseph was aware of all these events and promises and knew that he was one of those descendants, one of the inheritors of those promises. Many things happened to Joseph at Bethel and then on the journey to Migdal-eder and later Hebron.

📖 Read Genesis 35:16–21. How do you think these events might have impacted Joseph?

_____

_____

_____

_____

On the journey to Migdal-eder, Joseph's mother Rachel bore Benjamin, his full brother and Jacob's twelfth son. Benjamin would be very special to Joseph. But in giving birth, Rachel lost her life. The impact of the death of his mother when he was a young man would be significant, especially in light of the favored treatment Rachel and Joseph had received all his life. This would most likely make Joseph and Benjamin even more special to their father Jacob. (Note the name change from Ben-oni, "son of my sorrow," to Benjamin, "son of the right hand"—a place of special blessing.)

We tend to think of dysfunctional families as a problem unique to modern life, but Joseph's family shows us otherwise. People have always been people, with relationships complicated by the sin nature all of us bear. Joseph was born into a family whose complications rival those of many families today—including a step-mother, three sets of half-brothers, and the loss of his mother. It was a tangle of divided loyalties and resentments. Joseph could have easily become a victim of those circumstances, but he was learning from his father, Jacob, that he had a God bigger than any circumstances. In Genesis 37 we see that pressures in Joseph's life only intensify. There we see the full bloom of the brothers' attitudes and actions toward this favored son.

We have a God bigger than any circumstances.

📖 Read Genesis 37:1–11. How did Jacob set Joseph apart from his brothers?

_____

_____

What reasons did Joseph's brothers have for hating him (vv. 2, 4, 5)?

_____

_____

_____

_____

_____

Put Yourself In Their Shoes
THE FIRSTBORN

The rights and privileges of the first-born included headship of the family and a double inheritance. These rights could be passed to a younger child (usually the first-born of a later, more loved wife) until Moses made the practice illegal (Deuteronomy 2:15–17).

In Genesis 37, Joseph was seventeen years of age. He was very sensitive to right and wrong and did not mind speaking up about what he saw and knew. Jacob continued to show special love and care towards Joseph. He gave him the multi-colored tunic, a badge of honor usually reserved for the first-born. In this case the first-born, Reuben, had distinguished himself by his wickedness (35:22). Joseph, the eleventh son and Rachel's first-born, was honored instead. This made the brothers hate him. They could not get along with him or even speak on friendly terms. They had no wish for him to prosper in any way. To add to the distance, Joseph reported two dreams that indicated he would some day rule over them. This would fit with the fact that he already had the "ruler's" tunic given to him by Jacob. Little did Joseph realize the intensity of his brothers' resentment.

Joseph DAY TWO

FROM PIT TO PIT: SOMETIMES THE PRESSURES INCREASE

Joseph's report of his dreams and the gift of the multi-colored coat combined to intensify the jealousy of the brothers and increase their hatred for Joseph. Attitudes and feelings were bitter and at a boiling point. Then Joseph was sent by his father to "see about the welfare" of his brothers (37:14).

📖 Read the events of Genesis 37:18–24. What did Joseph's brothers do when they saw him coming?

_____

_____

_____

Read Genesis 42:21. How did he handle it?

_____

_____

When Joseph's brothers saw him coming, they mocked him as the "dreamer" and plotted to murder him. Reuben, the eldest, persuaded them not to kill him. They took his multicolored tunic, placed him in a pit and sat down to eat. Genesis 42:21 speaks of the "distress of his soul when he pleaded" with his brothers. He was in great distress, and they refused to listen. In Genesis 42:21 the word for *"distress"* literally means "tightness" and carries the idea of a "narrow or tight place," a "crowding in." Joseph was under pressure.

📖 Read Genesis 37:25–36. How did the circumstances Joseph faced intensify?

_____

_____

_____

_____

While the brothers were eating they noticed a caravan of Ishmaelite traders passing by on their way to Egypt, and they realized there was no profit in killing Joseph. Instead, they sold him for twenty pieces of silver. Reuben, who had been away from them, came back to the pit and found Joseph gone. At that point the brothers invented a cover-up story to tell their father. Jacob mourned for many days, and the brothers lived on in guilt (Genesis 42:22). The Midianites sold Joseph to Potiphar, captain of the Pharaoh's bodyguard.

Joseph had to have been confused about what God was allowing to happen in his life. He could have become bitter at his brothers and at God for allowing them to mistreat him. He could have focused his energy on waiting for God to rescue him in some way. He could have given up and settled into self-pity. But Joseph did none of those things. Instead he trusted God to be in control and did each next thing in such a way as to glorify God.

Joseph's life in Egypt began in slavery to Potiphar, captain of the Pharaoh's bodyguard. However, the most important thing was not where **Joseph** was, but where **God** was. And *"the LORD was with Joseph"* (39:2). As a result, Joseph prospered as a manager over Potiphar's household. This was evident to Potiphar, who recognized something of the presence and blessing of the Lord (39:3). Joseph became a personal servant to Potiphar, and his success continued for some time (39:4–6).

📖 Read Genesis 39:7–18. What pressure did Potiphar's wife put on Joseph?

_____

_____

How did he respond to this pressure?

_____

_____

_____

_____

What was the key to his response (v. 9)?

_____

_____

_____

Joseph was *"handsome in form and appearance"* (39:6), and Potiphar's wife *"looked with desire at Joseph"* (v. 7). She spoke with him day after day, but he

Did You Know?

THE MULTI-COLORED COAT

The coat given to Joseph by Jacob was probably a long tunic with sleeves worn by youths of the richer class. It was most likely reserved for the firstborn and signified position and honor. Joseph's brothers apparently resented Joseph's ownership of the coat itself, as well as the status it implied, since they made a point to strip him of it.

Joseph had a solid foundation of knowing right from wrong, and he had developed a personal relationship with God that gave him the power to make the right choices.

ignored her words and avoided her presence. When she sought to entrap him, Joseph ran from her and from the house. He was then falsely accused (vv. 13–18). The key to Joseph's response was his walk with the Lord. He had a heart-felt respect of God, a trust in Who He is and what He expects. He knew this was sin *("evil")* first against God, then against Potiphar and his wife. Despite the circumstances in his family, Jacob had evidently taught Joseph the ways of God. Joseph had a solid foundation of knowing right from wrong, and he had developed a personal relationship with God that gave him the power to make the right choices.

📖 Read Genesis 39:19–23. What pressures resulted because Joseph did the right thing?

_____

_____

Read Genesis 40:1–23. As time passed, what additional pressures did Joseph experience?

_____

_____

How did he respond (39:21–23, 40:14–15)?

_____

_____

Joseph faced the anger of Potiphar, as well as the reality of being falsely accused and labeled as an adulterer. In jail he interpreted the dreams of the cupbearer and the baker. But when the cupbearer was restored, he forgot about Joseph. Joseph knew the presence, kindness, and favor of the Lord during that time (v. 21), though he still faced the pressure of being in jail. In verse 15 he speaks of being kidnapped from the land of the Hebrews, of doing nothing unjust, and of being in the *"dungeon,"* literally the *"pit."* Joseph's speech is gracious in 40:14. There is no bitterness evident, and he never blames God.

We have seen that Joseph began this stage of his life (age seventeen) in a pit in great distress. Thirteen years later at age thirty (Genesis 41:46), he was in a "pit" again (translated *"dungeon"* in 40:15). Remember, the word for *"distress"* means tightness or crowded in, a good picture of life in a "pit." Psalm 46:1 uses the same word and translates it *"trouble."*

📖 Read Psalm 46. What does it say about how we should respond to pressures (vv. 1–3, 10)?

_____

_____

_____

Think back to Genesis 39 and 40. Was Joseph living in fear?

_____

Was he *"striving"*?

_____

APPLY How do you tend to react when you're in a tight spot or under pressure?

_____

_____

_____

According to Psalm 46, why are we not to fear or strive?

_____

_____

_____

When we are looking at the circumstances around us, they can be overwhelming. But God overwhelms every circumstance, and we can trust Him to see us through. Keeping our focus on God puts the worst of circumstances in perspective.

But God didn't intend to leave Joseph in the "pit" forever. The cupbearer did eventually remember him . . . two years later! (Genesis 41:1). And Joseph is summoned to the court to interpret Pharaoh's dream.

Read Genesis 41:14–16. Why did Pharaoh finally call for Joseph?

_____

_____

How did Joseph respond to this new pressure (v. 16)?

_____

_____

Genesis 41 gives us the account of how Joseph was called to interpret Pharaoh's dreams when all the _"wise men"_ of Egypt could not, and Pharaoh had heard that Joseph could. Here was a new pressure point. How did Joseph face it? In his meeting with Pharaoh, Joseph was quick to point out that _"it is not in me"_ (v. 16) to interpret the dreams. The focus of Joseph's thinking and of his response was God and His ability to guide correctly.

Verses 17 through 37 detail Pharaoh's dream and the interpretation Joseph revealed.

Read Genesis 41:25, 28, and 32. To whom did Joseph give all the credit?

_____

In verses 33–37, what did Joseph recommend to Pharaoh?

_____

_____

_____

In verses 16, 25, 28, and 32, God was at the center of all that was going on. Joseph was God-centered, and he testified in such a way that everyone understood clearly that he gave God all the credit for his abilities to interpret. After Joseph gave the interpretation of a coming seven years of abundance followed

> ## When we are looking at the circumstances around us, they can be overwhelming. But God overwhelms every circumstance, and we can trust Him to see us through.

by a seven year famine, he advised Pharaoh to select a wise and discerning man to manage the land of Egypt and prepare for the coming disaster.

📖 Read Genesis 41:38–45. How did Pharaoh respond to Joseph's recommendation?

_____

_____

_____

Why did Pharaoh put Joseph in such a high position (v. 39)?

_____

Pharaoh recognized that God was with Joseph, and that *"divine spirit"* made Joseph the man for the job. Pharaoh immediately made him second in command and gave him complete authority over the entire land. Joseph began to rule in the land of his slavery.

Joseph **DAY THREE**

SOMETIMES THE PRESSURE IS FOR OTHERS

Joseph ruled with wisdom and skill. During the time before the famine, he married and had two sons. The painful pressures of the pit had eased, but now there was a whole new pressure: the challenge of leadership. Joseph had the job of preparing a nation for coming disaster. How did he handle this new chapter in his life?

📖 Read Genesis 41:50–52. What do the names Joseph gave his sons mean?

Manasseh –_____

_____

Ephraim – _____

_____

What does this tell you about Joseph's attitude towards God and towards his past?

_____

_____

_____

> **Joseph recognized God's presence and saw God's hand at work. He was God-centered in the face of pressures.**

As Joseph reflected on the birth of his sons, his focus remained God-centered. He named his first son Manasseh, meaning "to cause to forget," because God had made him forget his days of trouble. In describing his days in slavery and jail as days of *"trouble,"* he used the Hebrew word that refers to heavy labor with the idea of unfulfilling labor and drudgery. God made him forget all those days. With the birth of his second son, Joseph chose the name Ephraim, meaning "doubly fruitful," because he saw that God had made him fruitful in a land where he had experienced much affliction. The word *"affliction"* has the idea of misery, of "looking down." Again, he recognized God's presence and saw God's hand at work. He was God-centered in the face of these pressures.

Genesis 41:53–57 tells how Joseph prepared the nation for the long famine. Verse 57 says that when the famine came, *"all the earth"* came to Joseph to buy grain because the famine was so widespread. God maneuvered Joseph into a place of prosperity in preparation for a time when others would know the pressure of need. From that place he was able to help many people.

What purpose does God give in 2 Corinthians 1:3–6 for our afflictions?

_____

_____

_____

Sometimes God guides us through times of pressure and comforts us there so that we will be in a position to help others and minister to them in their time of affliction. God wants to use us, and He will bring us through times of pressure to make us usable.

Genesis 42:1–5 tells of the pressures that came to Jacob and his family as the famine struck the land of Canaan. The sons did not know what to do. In Genesis 42:1 Jacob asked his sons, *"Why are you staring at one another?"* Apparently they were all perplexed and confused. The situation was not going well. Jacob mentioned the great need, *"that we may live and not die,"* and sent ten sons to Egypt. But he kept Benjamin at home because he was afraid he would come to harm. Jacob was still dealing with his sorrow over the loss of Joseph twenty-two years earlier.

When the brothers arrived in Egypt, Joseph recognized them and remembered the dreams he had as a young man (v. 9). At this point he felt compelled to test them.

Read Genesis 42:9–17. Why do you think Joseph tested them in this way?

_____

_____

_____

_____

Genesis 42:16 says Joseph wanted to test his brothers to see if there was truth in them. He knew they had been deceitful in many ways while he was growing up; therefore, he tested them.

The pressures the brothers were facing in Canaan had a purpose. Their journey to Egypt and coming before Joseph had a purpose as well. God was using this to fulfill His purposes for them and, through them, to bring about His purposes for the world. God certainly wanted Joseph reunited with Jacob. He had many wonderful plans for Jacob and his family, and He was at work in ways Jacob and Joseph could not see.

Sometimes on the journey we have to wait to clearly see the path which God has for us. When we do see the way He has taken us, we see the greatness of His wisdom and the wonder of His ways. Jacob and Joseph would see that. But sometimes we do not see or understand what is going on around us. That was certainly true of the ten brothers. It was also true of Jacob.

Did You Know?

JOSEPH'S RULE OF EGYPT

When the famine struck, the grain was sold to the people, first for money, then livestock, land, and eventually the servitude of the people themselves. All this came to Pharaoh. Joseph then bought up all the remaining land for Pharaoh (except that belonging to the priests, who were given an allotment of grain by Pharaoh), and distributed the people to the cities where the grain was stored. The people worked Pharaoh's land and paid him a tax of one-fifth of each harvest, a law which was still enforced at the time of the writing of the book of Genesis (chapter 47).

Sometimes on the journey we have to wait to clearly see the path which God has for us.

📖 Read Genesis 42:29–38 and 43:1–15. What was Jacob's perspective on what had transpired (42:36, 43:6, 12, 14)?

_____

_____

_____

_____

Like Jacob, we must often wait to see the bigger picture—the design God is working out for good.

The brothers returned from Egypt, and after they recounted their experiences in Egypt, Jacob concluded that *"all these things are against me."* He does not yet have the full picture; he sees the famine situation as all bad and even accuses his sons of treating him *"so badly."* Jacob hopes it was just a *"mistake,"* but he also realizes he may lose another son. Jacob is only considering what he can see. God was at work in ways Jacob did not know about at this point. But it doesn't appear that thought ever occurred to Jacob. He could have taken comfort that God was in control, but instead he suffered in anxiety.

📖 Read Genesis 43:16 through 44:17. When Joseph's brothers returned to Egypt with Benjamin, how did he test them once more?

_____

_____

_____

_____

Why do you think he tested them in this particular way?

_____

_____

When the brothers returned to Egypt with Benjamin, they passed Joseph's first test. But he must have remembered how much they had hated him and resented their father's favoritism. He wanted to see how much they had changed, if they would still be willing to risk their father's favorite for their own well-being. He had his own silver cup placed in Benjamin's bag of grain and sent his steward after them to accuse them of stealing it. When the cup was found, Joseph announced he would hold Benjamin as his slave.

📖 Read Genesis 44:18–34. How did the brothers respond to the test?

_____

_____

_____

The brothers had displayed no resentment towards Benjamin. Perhaps their father's grief upon losing Joseph had opened their eyes to their own selfishness and softened their hearts. Judah shows his love for his father by offering his own life in Benjamin's place.

📖 Read Genesis 45:1–15. What is Joseph's reaction (vv. 1–4)?

_____

_____

_____

In verses 5–7, what purpose does Joseph see in everything that has happened?

_____

_____

_____

_____

Who does Joseph say was behind it all (v. 8)?

_____

In verses 9–13, what message does Joseph send to his father?

_____

_____

_____

_____

Again we see Joseph's focus is on God. He recognizes God's hand in his life. He has walked in the fear of God, and recognized and acknowledged the hand of God working in his life and circumstances. Joseph sees that the pressures had a purpose—to *"preserve life,"* particularly that of his family. It was God, not the brothers, who brought him to Egypt, and He did so to accomplish His purposes for His people. Through Joseph, his father and brothers have been saved. The wonders of God's ways in guiding His people continued to unfold in and through the life of Joseph.

APPLY   Has anyone ever wronged you?

_____

How do you tend to respond in those situations? (Check the one that best describes you.)

____ I get angry and clam up.
____ I lash out in anger.
____ I recognize that God uses it for good.
____ I quietly plot revenge.
____ I act as if nothing ever happened.
____ My feelings get hurt and I sulk.
____ I try to remember that everybody is a victim.

How willing are you to see the hand of God in the evil others do to you? We tend to only want to see God's hand in the good things. If someone acts maliciously towards us, then we assume its affect on our lives must be a bad thing. In Joseph's life, this was obviously not the case; the evil act of his brothers resulted in great good, even through the pain and suffering Joseph endured. This evil that Joseph's brothers inflicted on him resulted in Joseph becoming a man of wealth and influence, a nation being prepared for famine, Joseph's family being saved from starvation, a reconciliation of family relationships, *"and the people of all the earth came to Egypt to buy grain from Joseph"* (Genesis 41:57). God is *always* sovereign and always working to accomplish His purpose in our lives and in the world.

> **Joseph has walked in the fear of God, and recognized and acknowledged the hand of God working in His life and circumstances.**

THE PURPOSES OF PRESSURE

While Joseph related the story of God's hand in his life to his family, he not only began to show his brothers the wonders of God's provision, but also something of the awesome ways of God, of the loving character and care of the Lord. Considering Joseph's dysfunctional family and his slavery in Egypt, he could have been miserable and bitter because of these pressures. Instead, he chose to be willing to be used by God, and therefore saw God's gracious provision and blessing in and through his life.

📖 Read Genesis 45:10–13 and verses 16–24. What tangible provision had God prepared for Jacob and his family through Joseph?

_____

_____

_____

_____

📖 Read Genesis 45:7–9. What does Joseph say about God's purposes in all that has occurred?

_____

_____

_____

_____

> *Joseph chose to be willing to be used by God, and therefore saw God's gracious provision and blessing in and through his life.*

Joseph showed great care for his brothers as he described to them how God had worked, even through their evil intentions. He made sure they understood that it was God's purpose of caring for them that brought all these circumstances together. Joseph will personally make sure his family is well provided for throughout the famine. And Pharaoh is so pleased that he promises them *"the best of all the land of Egypt."* They are even given everything they might need to make the journey.

It is truly a picture of how God cares for His children and provides for their tangible needs through pressures. But God also uses pressure to provide us with the less tangible things He knows we need: strong relationships with others and Himself.

📖 Read the following verses and list those intangible provisions Jacob sees given by God.

Genesis 45:25–28 _____

_____

Genesis 46:1–4 _____

_____

Genesis 48:15–16a _____

_____

Genesis 49:26 _____

_____

Jacob saw that the hand of God had preserved Joseph from harm—*"it is enough; my son Joseph is still alive."* God also promised him that Joseph would be with him until his death. In addition, he saw the provision of God's presence for the journey to Egypt and the eventual return. At the point of his death in Egypt, Jacob knew more than ever before that the God of Abraham and Isaac *"has been my shepherd all my life to this day"* (48:15). He also saw God redeem him *"from all evil"* (48:16) and bless him to the utmost (49:26).

God also used all the trials and pressures Joseph faced to bless him in great measure. The account of the blessing of his father Jacob is one of the most magnificent passages in Scripture.

📖 Read Genesis 49:22–26. How does Jacob describe the pressures Joseph had faced (v. 23)?

_____

_____

_____

According to verse 24, how did Jacob describe Joseph's response to those pressures?

_____

What does Jacob's blessing reveal about the character of God (vv. 24–26)?

_____

_____

_____

The names of God express His attributes. How have you seen these attributes at work in Joseph's life?

_____

_____

_____

_____

_____

> Jacob acknowledged God as "the God who has been my shepherd all my life to this day."
> Genesis 48:15

As *"archers bitterly attacked . . . and harassed him,"* Joseph stood firm. The Lord is revealed as *"the Mighty One of Jacob,"* giving him strength. We see *"the Shepherd"* guiding Joseph and *"the Stone of Israel"* providing stability. He is *"the God"* (El) of Jacob who helps by His might, and *"the Almighty"* (Shaddai) who blesses by His abundance. Jacob had seen those blessings in his life and in the account of Joseph's life. He wanted them to continue for Joseph, and so he blessed him before he died.

After Jacob's death the brothers were again concerned about their welfare under Joseph. Now that Jacob was dead, they feared their protection was gone. They were about to see just how real Joseph's faith in God was.

> **"And as for you, you meant evil against me, but God meant it for good in order to bring about this present result, to preserve many people alive."**
> **Genesis 50:20**

Did You Know?
JOSEPH'S BONES

In the Exodus from Egypt, Moses took the bones of Joseph with them, honoring his dying request (Genesis 50:25; Exodus 13:19). He was eventually buried in Shechem (Joshua 24:32).

📖 Read Genesis 50:15–21. How does Joseph respond to his brothers' worry (particularly vv. 17, 19, 21)?

_____

_____

_____

_____

What does Joseph say about God's purpose for his pressures (v. 20)?

_____

_____

Joseph urged them not to be afraid. He had not forgotten that it was God who had guided all along the way and had provided everything. Joseph knew he was not in God's place to judge. He was in the place God provided so that he could provide for, protect, and do good for God's people. (This is the same idea we saw in Genesis 2 when Adam was instructed to grow/provide, guard/protect life, and choose good in the Garden. God's design is the same for us.) Joseph had learned that, though they meant evil against him, God meant it all for good. The specific good was the preservation of Jacob's entire family and beyond that, the growth of a nation. We know from the rest of Scripture that this nation one day would give birth to the Messiah, the God-Man, the Savior of the world.

Sometimes God's purposes in our pressures may be far beyond anything we will ever see in this life. Many times He shows us the tangible results of His work in our lives, but whether we can see it clearly or not, He always has a purpose. His purpose is always good, acceptable, and perfect (Romans 12:2), and He is always working everything to the fulfillment of that purpose.

Joseph **DAY FIVE**

FOR ME TO FOLLOW GOD

Joseph had more pressure in his life than most of us can ever imagine. And this pressure came from every angle. Yet, we consistently see a response throughout Joseph's life that is uncomplaining, selfless, full of compassion, eager to serve whatever the circumstances, and marked by peace. He set a standard that looks daunting to any of us, and he did it without having the presence of the indwelling Holy Spirit in his life. We not only have everything that Joseph had that allowed him to respond that way, but the Holy Spirit's indwelling presence as well. So let's look at what made up Joseph's response and see how God wants to change us.

📖 Thinking back through this week's lessons, list the pressures Joseph faced throughout his life.

_____

_____

_____

_____

_____

APPLY What are some of the pressures you struggle with on a daily basis?

_____

_____

_____

_____

What is your typical response to those pressures?

_____

_____

The pressures you face every day may not look as bad as those Joseph faced, but God wants to teach us faithfulness even in the small things so that He can make us more usable in the larger ones. The small chips from His chisel have just as much purpose in conforming us to the image of His Son as the sledge hammer blows we at times experience. The circumstances are different, but the principles are the same. And it is those principles, those tools, that we can observe in Joseph's life and apply in our own.

Perhaps the most basic tool Joseph had that enabled him to deal with the pressures in his life was knowing God. Knowing God isn't some mystical, out of reach experience. What does it mean to know someone? You know the things that are characteristic of them: their likes and dislikes, the principles that determine their actions. You know their place in your life; the things you share with them. You know how much authority they have in your life and in what areas that authority extends. You know their attitude towards you; what they think about you and the things you do. God is not an obscure force, He is a person, and He wants us to know Him.

📖 Read Genesis 45:7–8. Who did Joseph know was in control of his life and all the pressures he faced?

_____

📖 According to Romans 12:2, what characterizes God's desires for us?

_____

_____

📖 Read Genesis 50:20. What did Joseph say about what God wanted for his life?

_____

_____

📖 Read John 3:16. What is God's personal motivation for His activity in your life?

_____

_____

We can know God because He has described Himself to us in His Word. As we read the Bible, we begin to recognize His character and ways He is at

> **God is not an obscure force; He is a person, and He wants us to know Him.**

work in our lives and the lives of those around us. We can know Him more and more as we read what He says and watch what He does. Our entire lives should be marked by an ever-increasing knowledge of God Himself. The next step, believing and trusting Him, flows naturally out of knowing God.

📖 Read Genesis 40:8, 12–14 and 41:15–16, 25, 33–36. How do these incidents show that Joseph believed and trusted God?

_____

_____

_____

_____

_____

Joseph knew what God expected of Him, so he was faithful to obey. And he knew that whatever the immediate consequences, God would be faithful to honor that obedience.

📖 In Genesis 37:5–11, we read about two dreams Joseph had which implied that his family would bow down to him. What do you think the seventeen year old Joseph might have expected in his life because of those dreams?

    ___ respect   ___ accomplishment
    ___ position   ___ prestige
    ___ comfort   ___ love
    ___ acclaim   ___ honor

When instead he experienced abuse, hatred, slavery, humiliation and hardship, we never see him complain. Joseph died to his own agenda and comfort. He lived a life marked by denying himself for the sake of God and of others.

📖 Read Matthew 6:25–34. What do you know about God's character from these verses (vv. 26, 30, 32)?

_____

_____

And what should our response be (vv. 33–34)?

_____

_____

_____

_____

If God is trustworthy, then we must trust Him completely. We often limit what God wants to do in our lives because we are afraid—afraid of pain, suffering, or disappointment. We're really afraid that what God wants for us might not really be the best. We should know God better than that.

Joseph had heard the words of God from his father, and he had watched God work in his own life as well as the lives of others around him. He knew God, and because God is who He is, Joseph trusted Him with his life. He

> Joseph knew what God expected of him, so he was faithful to obey. He knew that whatever the immediate consequences, God would be faithful to honor that obedience.

accepted everything in his life as from God's hand, and did whatever work God placed before him.

No matter what his circumstances were, Joseph was not controlled by them. He knew Who was in control of those circumstances, and he survived and prospered by following God. Joseph went through the worst in his life, but he experienced the best because he consistently relied on the faithfulness of God. That is the essence of following God.

We've seen in Joseph's life the benefits of knowing and trusting God. We've discussed what it means to get to know Him, so how do we build that relationship with God?

1. We should recognize that God is worth knowing personally;
2. We should read the book He wrote to reveal Himself to us, seeking Him in His Word; and
3. We should open ourselves up to Him in prayer, making Him our most familiar and trusted friend.

Spend some time in prayer with the Lord right now.

 Lord, forgive me for the self-pity I at times allow to rule my life. Nothing comes to me that has not been measured out by Your loving hand. Help me to live in the reality that You control every circumstance of my life, and change the attitude of my heart to accept that You use every circumstance for Your purpose. I want to recognize Your blessings in all things, not just in pleasant conditions. Teach me to follow faithfully in times of discomfort and trial, every day trusting You and doing whatever You have placed before me. I want to know You Lord, and in knowing You, to be conformed to Your image. In Jesus' name, Amen.

Write out your prayer to the God of all comforts.

_____

_____

_____

_____

_____

_____

_____

_____

_____

_____

_____

_____

Moses

PRACTICING THE PRESENCE OF GOD

One of the greatest assurances in the Christian life is the promised presence of God. He has stated it emphatically in both the Old and New Testaments. The writer of Hebrews 13:5, speaking from the words of Moses and Joshua, states, *"He Himself has said, 'I will never desert you, nor will I ever forsake you.'"* The promise that Moses, Joshua, and hundreds of other Old Testament saints knew carried them through life. We have an even greater promise in that the Person of the Holy Spirit is not only with us but also in us. Moses learned much about the ways and character of God as he walked in God's presence, especially in the last forty years of his life. From the example and words of Moses we can learn much about following God and knowing His presence.

Moses had the promise of God's presence. We have an even greater promise—the Person of the Holy Spirit is not only with us but also in us!

WHERE DOES HE FIT?

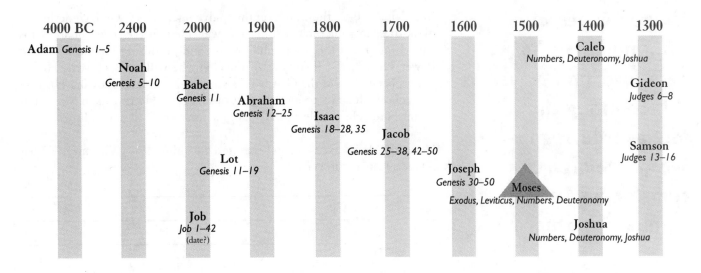

4000 BC	2400	2000	1900	1800	1700	1600	1500	1400	1300

Adam *Genesis 1–5*

Noah *Genesis 5–10*

Babel *Genesis 11*

Abraham *Genesis 12–25*

Isaac *Genesis 18–28, 35*

Jacob *Genesis 25–38, 42–50*

Lot *Genesis 11–19*

Joseph *Genesis 30–50*

Job *Job 1–42* (date?)

Caleb *Numbers, Deuteronomy, Joshua*

Gideon *Judges 6–8*

Samson *Judges 13–16*

Moses *Exodus, Leviticus, Numbers, Deuteronomy*

Joshua *Numbers, Deuteronomy, Joshua*

"I AM" WILL BE WITH YOU

The Hebrew for "Moses" is *mosheh,* which means "drawn out." But the original is Egyptian, *mase,* meaning "a child or a son." This was a common element of many Egyptian names. Basically, Pharaoh's daughter simply called him "the child."

Exodus chapters 1 and 2 tell the story of Moses from his birth to the age of about eighty. Read that passage to familiarize yourself with his background. (You may also want to look at Hebrews 11:23–27 and Acts 7:18–29.) In Exodus 3, we find the Lord appearing to him in the burning bush. The adventure of following God was beginning.

Read Exodus 3:1–9. In your own words, list at least six things that God tells Moses in these verses.

_____

_____

_____

_____

_____

Exodus 3:4 reveals that God came to Moses. He initiated the call to him. God revealed Himself as holy, and the very ground where He manifested Himself was to be treated as holy (v. 5). God revealed Himself as the covenant-making and covenant-keeping God of Abraham, Isaac, and Jacob. God's presence brought fear to Moses. Moses knew the power and character of the Lord God (v. 6). God made it clear that He fully understood the suffering of His people in Egypt and heard their cry (v. 7). He was acting to deliver them out of Egypt and into Canaan, a land flowing with milk and honey (v. 8). God wanted Moses to fully understand His care, His response to Israel's cry, and His clear commitment to deal with their oppression (v. 9).

Carefully read Exodus 3:10–22, and mark all the references to God (I, I AM, He, My, God, Lord). What is God telling Moses about Himself in these verses?

_____

_____

_____

Practicing the presence of God is . . . living by faith in the fact that God Himself is personally with me in His holiness, love, and power. It is counting that fact as true, regardless of feelings, circumstances, or the opinions of others.

In Exodus 3:10–22 there are over thirty-five references to God. Underline or mark these in your Bible text in some way. He is at the center of all that is happening. He is the one sending Moses and promising His Presence and Power. He is *"I AM WHO I AM,"* the God who will always be who He has always been. This is the God who is sending Moses and showing His care and concern for His people. As part of His plan, He reveals to Moses His promises for His people and His judgments which will fall on Egypt.

Note that Moses' excuse in 3:11 is centered on himself—"Who am I?" What is God's response in verse 12?

_____

_____

_____

APPLY What does God's response tell you about who you are and God's relationship to you?

_____

_____

_____

_____

_____

GOD'S PROMISE, GOD'S PRESENCE

God promises Moses _"I will be with you...."_ Remember, it is God who is sending Moses. Because God is with Moses, he will bring God's people out of Egypt. God is not focused on who Moses is. God is focused on who He is, how adequate He is, and on the calling and responsibility of His people to worship Him as the one true God.

📖 Read Exodus 4:1–9. What is God's response to Moses' excuse in verse one?

_____

_____

_____

Why do you think God did not directly answer Moses' question?

_____

_____

_____

APPLY How does God respond to the "what if's" we bring up when we are asked to follow Him?

_____

_____

_____

> **"I will be with you...."**
> **Exodus 3:12**

When Moses heard what God wanted him to do, Moses began to bring up "what if's" to God. God proved His power and His presence in the incidents of the staff becoming a serpent and changing back to a staff, and Moses' hand becoming leprous and then made whole again. He promised that if they did not believe those two signs, He would turn the water of the Nile to blood before them.

God was making it very clear that He would be faithful. Moses could count on Him. God is patient with the doubts and concerns of the heart truly seeking Him. Following God is a life-long journey, and He doesn't expect us to have "arrived" overnight. He is faithful to give us the light and direction we need one step at a time.

📖 Moses offered more excuses in Exodus 4:10 and 4:13. Note carefully God's responses in 4:11–12 and 4:14–17. What does God say about His presence and character in these responses?

_____

_____

_____

How should Moses (or you) respond to God's direction?

_____

_____

_____

Moses had to deal with his stubborn self-will to begin realizing the riches of God's presence.

In response to Moses' excuse about not being eloquent in speech God promised, _"I, even I_ [emphatic construction], _will be with your mouth, and teach you what you are to say."_ God promised His presence for every circumstance, every conversation, every response that was needed. When Moses was still resistant, God's anger burned against Moses, and He commanded him to speak through his brother Aaron. Again God promised, _"I, even I, will be with your mouth and his mouth, and I will teach you what you are to do."_ Here, the promise was not only for what he should say but included all he was _"to do"_ (compare verses 12 [_"say"_] and 15 [_"do"_]). God was making sure Moses understood the scope of His promises and what His presence would mean in everything He had called him to do. It meant it would get done.

📖 God wanted Moses to go forth with confidence, knowing God would be with him. Read Exodus 4:2–5. Why would Moses have been carrying a staff?

_____

_____

_____

What did God tell him to do with the staff, and what happened when he did it?

_____

_____

_____

What does Exodus 4:17 tell you about the purpose of the staff?

_____

_____

_____

In verse 20, Moses is leaving his previous lifestyle behind, but he takes the staff with him. What does this say about how Moses had come to perceive the staff?

_____

_____

_____

The Lord instructed Moses to take the staff as the instrument by which he would perform the needed signs that would convince others of God's presence and power. That staff belonged to Moses. God commanded it to be thrown down. Moses obeyed. He released it to God, who then directed Moses to pick it up once again after it had become a serpent. It became a staff again. Exodus 4:20 makes it clear that it was then *"the staff of God."* It had been handed over to God. He took possession of it and would use it in Moses' hand to reveal Himself. It was a symbol of the presence, the authority, and the power of God.

Often the things we have—gifts, talents, strength, or abilities—are not useful to God until we give Him possession of them. We may even think that we are serving Him with them, but we have no comprehension of the powerful work He will do through us until we hand them over to Him.

With Moses' excuses out of the way and his confidence in the presence and power of God, Moses and Aaron went to the people of Israel and then to Pharaoh. God revealed Himself in power in every instance. Through the Ten Plagues, Pharaoh and Egypt found out about the power and authority of the God of Israel. Each plague was a refutation to a specific Egyptian god. The Nile was considered sacred and blessed by the gods, Khnum (protector of the Nile) and Hapi (or Apis, the bull god). Frogs represented Heqet (goddess of birth) who had a frog's head. The plague of lice or gnats from dust represented Set (god of the desert) and could have been an affront on the ritual purity of Egyptian priests who would have been defiled by the presence of these pests. The plague of flies may have been Ichneuman flies, representative of the god Uatchit. The death of livestock was an affront to the goddess Hathor, described as a woman with a cow's head, or to Apis (the bull god). The boils struck at Sekhmet (goddess who supposedly could heal disease), Sunu (god of pestilence), and Isis (goddess of life). The plagues of hail and locusts stood in stark opposition to Nut (goddess of the sky), and Set and Osiris (protectors of crops). The plague of darkness stood against Re and Horus (sun gods) as well as Nut. The death of the firstborn was an affront to Pharaoh who, along with his son, was considered a god, to Isis, the goddess the Egyptians thought protected their children, and to Osiris, the "giver of life." God revealed Himself in great strength and power. His presence with Moses and the children of Israel during these plagues was just the beginning of the revelation of the one true God, who promised His presence to His chosen people and their leaders Moses and Aaron.

Moses and the people of Israel began to learn some vital lessons about the presence of God in their midst and what that meant. We will see more about that in Day Three.

> **Did You Know?**
> ### THE TEN PLAGUES
> ### EXODUS 7:14—12:33
>
> 1. Nile River turned to blood
> 2. Frogs
> 3. Gnats or lice
> 4. Flies
> 5. Livestock died from disease
> 6. Boils
> 7. Hail
> 8. Locusts
> 9. Darkness
> 10. Death of the firstborn
>
> *Each plague was a refutation to a specific Egyptian god. At each point the presence and power of the Lord was clearly seen to be victorious over every god the Egyptians worshiped.*

MOSES IN GOD'S PRESENCE

Moses **DAY THREE**

The people of Israel discovered the faithfulness of their covenant-God, the God of Abraham, Isaac, and Jacob. They saw the Lord deliver them through the Passover, the parting of the Red Sea, and through many wilderness trials. At Mount Sinai God revealed Himself in even greater power and authority as their God. He gave them the Law, the Priesthood, the Tabernacle, the Laws of the Offerings and the Feasts and reminded them of His promises of a home in Canaan. The people promised obedience but failed time after time in those few months. Did God abandon them? What happened in Moses' life? What can we learn about His presence in Moses' life and in the lives of the people in the midst of the Wilderness?

How did God reveal His presence in Exodus 13:17–22, and what does that say about His faithfulness?

_____

_____

_____

God was faithful to go with them. He was seen in the pillar of cloud by day and in the pillar of fire by night. At all times and in all places He was leading, caring, and providing for the people.

The Tabernacle was to be at the center of all that Israel did once they left Mount Sinai. What was the purpose of the Tabernacle according to Exodus 25:8 and 22?

_____

_____

_____

The Lord wanted to dwell with or dwell among the people of Israel through the vessel known as the Tabernacle. It was to be constructed as a *"sanctuary for Me."* Exodus 25:22 reveals that God desired to *"meet with"* and *"speak to"* Moses and the people in the temple. It is evident that God wanted not only Moses, but also His people, to know and experience His presence continuously.

While Moses was on the mountain with God receiving the law and plans for the Tabernacle, the guidelines for true worship and fellowship, the people chose to enter into false worship around a golden calf (Exodus 32:1–6). The Lord was angry (vv. 7–10), and when Moses saw their folly, his anger burned (vv. 15–35). He dealt with their sin, and about three thousand men died that day. In Exodus 33:1–3 the Lord stated that He would see that the people got to the Promised Land, but He would not go in their midst because of their stubborn, obstinate ways. Instead, He would send an angel before them. This was a sad revelation, but it did not end there.

What was Moses' habit as they went from Egypt through the Wilderness according to Exodus 33:7–11?

_____

_____

_____

Moses pitched a tent, *"the tent of meeting,"* outside the camp. This was not the Tabernacle, but a separate place for seeking the Lord. When Moses went there the Lord met him in the pillar of cloud. There the Lord spoke with Moses *"face to face,"* meaning a very close relationship as friend to friend. But God had distanced Himself from His people because of their stubborn and obstinate ways.

📖 Read Exodus 33:12–13. Moses was confident that God knew him, and he pleaded with God to go with them, to let them know His presence

Word Study
TABERNACLE

The Hebrew word *bayith* (used for the Tabernacle in Exodus 23:19; 34:26; Joshua 6:4; 9:23; Judges 18:31; 20:18) has the basic meaning of "house." It is used in the compound word, *beth-el*, meaning "the house of God," which was used by Jacob to name the place he first encountered God. The New Testament word for house, *oikos*, is found in I Timothy 3:15, within the context of *"the household of God, which is the church of the living God. . . ."*

throughout the journey to Canaan. What was God's two-fold response to Moses in 33:14?

_____

_____

_____

What was Moses' response in 33:15–16?

_____

_____

_____

God promised His presence and His rest. Moses wanted no part of a journey without the presence of God. The presence of God was the distinguishing mark of the people of God. He made all the difference in the world—*"upon the face of the earth."*

God also revealed Himself in His glory and goodness in Exodus 33:17–23 and 34:1–7. Moses worshiped the Lord there on Mount Sinai and asked once again for the Lord to go with them throughout their journey. He knew that the presence of God was the greatest gift and blessing they could have.

APPLY Briefly write out any times in your life when you were willing to go ahead without God.

_____

_____

_____

_____

Has His presence become the one and only thing you will not do without? Take a moment and pray, asking Him to make that a reality in your life.

God's Presence at Kadesh-Barnea

Moses DAY FOUR

> *Moses discovered that the presence of God was the one essential, the one necessity that made life what it was meant to be.*

God was faithful to take the children of Israel to the doorway of Canaan. At Kadesh-Barnea the Lord instructed Moses to send a leader from each of the twelve tribes to go in and spy out the land of Canaan—its people, its fruit, its cities, all that was there—and bring back a report of what the Lord was giving them. They did so, but ten of the twelve spies brought a bad report. They could see only defeat and destruction ahead. They did not believe the promises of God. They did not consider the powerful presence of God with them. The other two spies, Joshua and Caleb, saw things from God's perspective. What was the difference? What had they learned through Moses along the journey?

📖 Read Numbers 13:25–33; 14:1–4. How did the people respond to the report from the ten spies?

_____

_____

📖 Now look carefully at Numbers 14:5–9. Why were Joshua and Caleb confident?

_____

_____

That's what faith is . . . taking God at His word.

What did Joshua and Caleb see as the real danger?

_____

_____

Extra Mile

GOD'S PRESENCE AND JOSHUA

Read Joshua 1:1–9, and consider God's command and counsel to Joshua? Moses' practice of the presence of God had a strong impact on Joshua and Caleb. The fact that the Lord speaks of His presence with Moses shows that Joshua was fully aware of how crucial the Lord's presence was for every day, in every place, in every relationship, and for every task.

Read through Joshua 2—5, looking for the evidences of God's presence and what difference it made. What impact do you see? Do you see any personal applications?

Joshua and Caleb saw with their own eyes the truth about how good the land was, just as God had promised. They knew God had promised to give them the land. To Joshua and Caleb, unbelief in the promises of God was rebellion, disobedience, and fear of man. The people were not honoring God. Joshua and Caleb saw that the Lord had removed the protection from the people of Canaan. They would be *"prey"* (literally, "food") for the people of God. For Joshua and Caleb, the cry of the people should have been, *"The LORD is with us; do not fear them."* That was the basis of their confidence: the powerful presence of God.

In Numbers 14:11–12 the Lord was ready to smite the people and start over with Moses and his descendants. Moses began to intercede for the people. The basis of his prayer was the character and reputation of the Lord. God's presence among His people was well known to the nations around Canaan. Moses pled for the lovingkindness of the Lord to be shown once more. God did that. He left the nation alive by allowing those twenty years of age and younger to go into the Promised Land after forty years of wandering in the Wilderness. All the rest, except Joshua and Caleb, would die before that time.

📖 Read Numbers 14:39–45. What two things did the people finally realize (vv. 39–40)?

___They had misunderstood God.

___They had sinned against God.

___God wanted them to take the initiative.

___God had promised them the land.

___God's presence was with them.

In verses 41–43, what did Moses twice tell the people, and why would God not be with them?

_____

_____

_____

Thinking back, why had they turned back from following God? Why didn't they trust God? (For insight, read Proverbs 3:5–6.)

_____

_____

_____

In Numbers 14:42–43, Moses told the sinful, yet mournful Israelites not to ascend the ridge of the hill country to receive the promised land that the Lord had now denied them. What did the people do after Moses warned them? What did they go without? (Read vv. 44–45.)

_____

_____

_____

_____

God originally told the people to go in and conquer the land, and now that's what they were finally willing to do. So why did they fail?

_____

_____

_____

The people were willing to follow a formula of obedience, but they still refused to follow God. God is far more interested in a relationship with Him that results in trust and obedience, than a form of obedience based on our own understanding.

While the people mourned over Moses' words about the fact that they would not enter the land of Canaan and that they would die in the wilderness, they still ignored the word from the Lord and the warning of Moses. The next morning they prepared to conquer Canaan. Moses told them, *"The LORD is not among you."* He warned that the Amalekites and Canaanites would defeat them without the Lord's presence—*"The LORD will not be with you"* (v. 43). They ignored all he said. *"But they went up heedlessly,"* without **1)** the presence of the Lord, **2)** the ark of the covenant (the symbol of their covenant dependence and obedience), and **3)** the leadership of Moses. They suffered a humiliating defeat and ran away. The people had no regard or respect for the Lord, His Word, His leaders, or His presence. They thought they could do things their way. They were not following God. They were following the desires, thoughts, and opinions of their own hearts.

FOR ME TO FOLLOW GOD

Following God involves actively practicing His presence.

Moses DAY FIVE

What have you seen about walking in the presence of God, about practicing the presence of God? Think back to what God revealed to Moses about being with him and being with his mouth to speak whatever was needed. Think about the name "I AM WHO I AM." One of the application truths in that name can be phrased "I WILL BE WHO I HAVE BEEN."

With that thought in mind, how would you explain what it means to practice God's presence in your everyday life?

_____

_____

Are you practicing God's presence in your daily life?

_____

_____

_____

_____

 Think about Moses' excuses in Exodus 3 and 4. Are there any excuses that are keeping you from doing God's will? Is there a "staff" you are holding on to? Is there anything in your hand that needs to be thrown down, given to God, controlled, and owned by Him?

_____

_____

_____

_____

Are you walking with a confidence in God, or are you fearful, dismayed, or anxious because of disappointing circumstances or personal weaknesses?

 Which of the following best characterize your daily life? (Be honest with God and yourself. What does your spouse or closest friend see in you?)

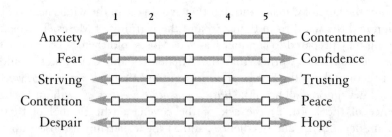

	1	2	3	4	5	
Anxiety	□	□	□	□	□	Contentment
Fear	□	□	□	□	□	Confidence
Striving	□	□	□	□	□	Trusting
Contention	□	□	□	□	□	Peace
Despair	□	□	□	□	□	Hope

Now that you're looking at where you are living, are you willing to let God change your life? Only then can others be aware of the presence of God because of you, your lifestyle, and your walk with God. (See Exodus 33:15–16.)

Are you following God, knowing and practicing His presence? That is the reason He created and recreated you. He wants you to walk with Him enjoying His presence and following His ways.

Spend some time in prayer with the Lord right now.

 O God and Father, I repent of my sinful preoccupation with visible things. The world has been too much with me. You have been there, and I knew it not. I have been blind to Your presence. Open my eyes, that I may behold You in and around me. I would dwell with You in daily experience here on this earth so that I may be accustomed to the glory when I enter Your heaven to dwell with You there. In Jesus' name. Amen.

A. W. Tozer

Write out your prayer. Remind yourself of His presence and thank Him for it.

_____

_____

_____

_____

_____

_____

_____

_____

_____

_____

Notes

Caleb

FOLLOWING GOD FULLY

Faith is taking God at His word, and it is that faith which marks the life of Caleb. As a result of his faith, God the Almighty, the Most Holy, said of Caleb, *"he has followed the LORD fully"* (Deuteronomy 1:36).

Caleb was a foreigner by birth. His father, Jephunneh the Kenizzite, was outside the circle of God's chosen people. Yet Numbers 14:24 states that he had *"a different spirit,"* and because of this, God used him mightily and honored him greatly. Because he was trustworthy and a recognized leader of his tribe, Judah, he was selected as one of the twelve spies sent in to investigate the promised land after the exodus from Egypt. He and Joshua advised the nation of Israel to follow God in obedience and possess the land. But the other ten warned of giants in the land, and Israel shrunk back in fear. The nation's unwillingness to follow the Lord into the promised land cost Israel forty years of wandering in the wilderness, during which that entire generation perished save Joshua and Caleb. By the time Israel entered the land of promise, Caleb was old in years but not weak in valor. God rewarded his faith by giving him the hill country as his prize. We want to scrutinize the life of this faithful man and see what we can learn from his faith.

Faith is taking God at His word, and it is that faith which marks the life of Caleb.

WHERE DOES HE FIT?

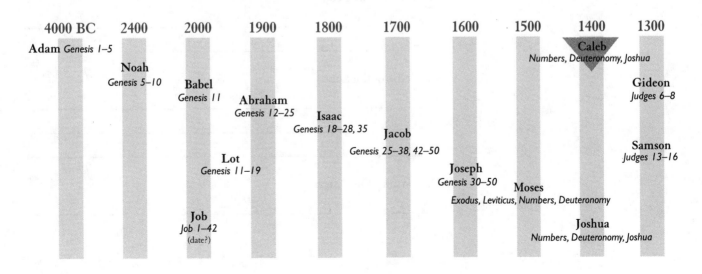

STANDING ON THE BORDERS OF BLESSING

The Exodus brought to an end four hundred years of toil and slavery in Egypt. Israel has just seen the power of God manifested in unique and dramatic ways through the plagues in Egypt and the parting of the Red Sea. They have seen God's supernatural provision for their needs with water from the rock and manna from heaven. God has visited them and given the law to them through Moses, and has established the Tabernacle as a means of worship. Now at Kadesh-Barnea they stand poised to enter the land God promised to Abraham, Isaac, and Jacob. Although Israel has never ceased believing in God, they have had their seasons of difficulty in trusting God. As they prepare to enter the promised land, we will see both heroes and villains. We want to look at the spies sent into Canaan and the role Caleb played. This will help us learn more about faith and faithfulness.

📖 Read Numbers 13:1–6. Why were Caleb and the other men selected to represent their tribes?

_____

_____

What does God say about the land they are to investigate?

_____

_____

Verse 2 indicates Moses was to select a leader from each of the twelve tribes of Israel (v. 3 reveals the men selected were the "*heads*" of the tribes). Each man would represent his tribe and report back what was seen in the land. It is significant that Caleb is to represent the tribe of Judah from whom the Messiah would eventually come. Notice what God says of this land: He calls it the land "*which I am going to give to the sons of Israel*" (v. 2). The outcome of the conquest was not in question—God had promised to give them the land.

📖 Read Numbers 13:17–24. What were the spies to look for while in the land?

Concerning the People:

1. _____

2. _____

Concerning the Land:

1. _____

2. _____

3. _____

Concerning the Cities:

_____

Did You Know?

HOW LONG SHOULD THE WILDERNESS JOURNEY HAVE LASTED?

Biblical scholars disagree on exactly how long the journey from Egypt to Canaan should have taken. Some believe the trip could have been made in as little as three days, while others suggest that it would have been more like a ten or eleven day trip. Whatever the case, because of Israel's unfaithfulness in following the Lord, it ended up being a forty-year journey. Often God's plans in our lives takes much longer than it should because we fail to follow Him.

Moses instructed them to make careful observations. Were the people strong or weak, few or many? Was the land good or bad, fat or lean? Was it full of trees, or not? Were the cities open and un-walled or strongly fortified? These were the things they needed to know as they approached conquering the land.

📖 According to Numbers 13:25–33, when the spies returned from their forty-day mission, what did the majority report?

Concerning the people?

_____

_____

Concerning the land?

_____

_____

Concerning the cities?

_____

_____

Concerning themselves in the land?

_____

_____

Did You Know?

MILK AND HONEY

What does it take to have a land that *"flows with milk and honey"*?

• Plenty of livestock—goats, cows, and sheep.

• Many grasses, hay, and straw.

• Water—wells, streams, and springs.

• Lots of bees.

• Many flowering trees, bushes, wild-flowers, and gardens.

All this was provided by the Lord.

When the men returned, all of them agreed that it was a land flowing with *"milk and honey."* They even brought back some of the abundant fruit of the land to show the people. But they also said it was a land of a strong people including giants, and that their cities were fortified. Most of the spies concluded that the people of the land were too strong for the people of Israel.

📖 Now look again at Numbers 13:25–33, and notice the context of Caleb's report in verse 30. Why did he speak up?

_____

_____

What did he have to say?

_____

_____

Verse 30 states that Caleb *"quieted the people before Moses."* Apparently grumbling and murmuring had overtaken the assembly. Caleb is speaking to counter the negative turn the report had taken as the spokesman focused on the human impossibility of the task. It seems that Caleb is the only one at this point who can see beyond the obstacles and keep the Lord in view. His minority report is the only exhortation to trust and obey the Lord's directive. It is significant that at this point there is no record of Joshua standing with Caleb. Although Joshua is more familiar to us, Caleb was the one leading here.

FAITH IS THE VICTORY

Even though they have seen God work miracle after miracle during the Exodus from Egypt, Israel still does not follow Him in trust and faith. Many times faith seems to stand alone, as Caleb and Joshua stood alone against the other spies and the people of Israel. But it is critical to remember that God always stands with the man or woman of faith. Being with God brings complete victory. Living without Him always results in utter defeat.

📖 Review Numbers 13:25–33. As we look at the report of the spies, it almost seems as if Caleb went somewhere different from the rest of the group. On what did the majority of the spies focus?

_____

_____

_____

Why do you think Caleb's perspective was so unlike theirs?

_____

_____

_____

Being with God brings complete victory. Living without Him always results in utter defeat.

Notice in verse 31, the spies say, *"**We** are not able . . ."* and *". . . they are too strong for **us**"* (emphasis added). There is no mention of what God is able to do. Their faithlessness even stains their view of the land itself. They begin by describing it as a land that flows with milk and honey, but in verse 32 all they can say is that it *"devours its inhabitants."* In verse 33 we see that failing to focus on God stains even their view of themselves. When they compare themselves with the giants, they begin to view themselves as grasshoppers, and they lose faith. Caleb's perspective, however, resulted in a response of faith because his focus was on the eternal God and His promises.

📖 In Numbers 14:1–2, how do the people respond to the reports of Caleb and the other spies?

_____

_____

The people responded in fear as if they hadn't heard Caleb at all, claiming it would have been better if they had died in Egypt or the Wilderness.

📖 According to Numbers 14:2–4, who did they blame for their apparent circumstances?

_____

_____

The people *"grumbled against Moses and Aaron"* and blamed God for leading them to slaughter.

When circumstances seem to be against you, do you typically respond in fear or in faith? Fear looks around itself and is overwhelmed. Faith looks at God and overcomes. In your life, which of these most often describes you?

___ Victim of my circumstances

___ Victor over my circumstances

Often we speak of faith as if it is some mystical endowment that a select few people have possessed throughout history, but that doesn't seem relevant to most of us in our day-to-day lives. We'd like to have the faith of a saint like Abraham or Caleb, but we assume that unless we are hit by some holy zap, it won't be available to people like us. But faith is not a mystical blessing for the few. Rather, it is fundamental to all believers and must be exercised. Faith is like a muscle—it grows with use and atrophies if it is not used. Faith is not a feeling, it is an often-made choice—it is the decision to take God at His word and place more of a value on what He says than on how things look from where we sit. It is not looking at what we can do for God, but rather at what He says He will do. It is this choice that sets Caleb apart.

In Numbers 14:1–4 we saw the congregation of Israel react in fear to the report and even begin to speak of appointing someone in Moses' place to lead them back to the slavery of Egypt.

📖 Read Numbers 14:6. How did Caleb and Joshua respond when Israel rebelled against Moses?

_____

_____

What did they say to the people in verses 7–9?

_____

_____

_____

_____

According to verse 10, how did the people respond to this?

_____

_____

When the people revolt, we see that Joshua stands with Caleb and the two of them tear their robes (a sign of mourning) and together rebuke the congregation, warning them not to rebel against the Lord (going into the land was a command, not a suggestion). For this, the people prepare to stone them, and only a visitation from God spares the lives of the two faithful leaders.

📖 Looking at Numbers 14:22–35, what consequence was the nation to suffer because of their choice?

_____

_____

> *Faith is an often-made choice—it is the decision to take God at His word and place more of a value on what He has to say than on how things look from where we sit.*

God says that the men (identified in 14:29 as all males twenty years old and older who had been numbered as soldiers) who had seen His power in Egypt but refused to trust would never get to see the Promised Land. In addition, God promises that any others who *"spurned"* the Lord, presumably referring to the women, would incur the same judgment.

As punishment for their unfaithfulness, Israel is sentenced to one year of wandering for each of the forty days the spies spent in the land. Of the spies, Numbers 14:36–38 tells us the ten-man majority, who made the congregation grumble by bringing a bad report, died immediately via a plague from the Lord.

In their complaint against God, Israel said, *". . . would that we had died in this wilderness!"* (Numbers 14:2). Jehovah turns their words against them as their judgment saying, *"just as you have spoken in My hearing, so I will surely do to you."* (Numbers 14:28). He promises that the men (who, as the God-ordained leaders of the home, always bear the greater responsibility) would all die in the wilderness, and their families would suffer for their unfaithfulness until all of those men were dead. Sin always has consequence.

📖 What, according to verses 24 and 30, were the consequences for Caleb because of his choice?

_____

_____

Caleb is credited in verse 4 with having *"a different spirit"* (a spirit of trust) and with following the Lord fully. He would outlive the judgment even though he would also join in the forty years of wandering. As a reward for his faith and faithfulness, he would be allowed to take possession of the land, and his descendants would share this blessing.

The choices we make always affect others around us, especially our children. Our children share in the blessings of God in our lives as well as in the consequences of our wrong choices. But this also means that we often have to live with the consequences of others' wrong choices. Caleb suffered for forty years because of the unbelief of others, but God's faithfulness to Him was unchanged.

🛑 **APPLY** Are there times in your life when you have suffered the consequences of someone else's unbelief or wrong choice?

_____

_____

_____

_____

Do you trust God's faithfulness to you in these situations, or have you become embittered toward those who are not trusting God? Describe how you usually respond when you find yourself in these kinds of situations.

_____

_____

_____

FORTY YEARS LATER

Just before reaching the Promised Land, Moses had taken a census of Israel. Every male twenty years old and upward who was able to go out to war was numbered. These men were the recognized leaders of Israel, and when they chose not to obey the Lord, refusing to go into the land, they were held accountable. God promised each would die in the Wilderness. Nearly forty years have passed, and plague after plague has befallen Israel because of their rebellion and disobedience.

📖 Read Numbers 25:1–3. Nearing the end of their forty years of wandering, has Israel learned to follow God?

_____

What were they doing?

_____

_____

_____

Israel was *"playing the harlot"* with the people of Moab, worshiping Baal with them.

How does God tell Moses to respond (vv. 4–5)? What was the result (v. 9)?

_____

_____

_____

_____

God tells Moses to execute the leaders of the people in broad daylight for all to see. Twenty-four thousand die in this *"plague"* of judgment over Baal worship. Now God calls Moses to a new census.

📖 Read Numbers 26:1–2. Considering that God had promised that all the men of the first census would die except Caleb and Joshua, what do you think is significant about the second census coming after a *"plague"*?

_____

_____

Word Study
PLAGUE

The Hebrew word translated "plague" in Numbers 25 is *maggephah*. It means "a blow, slaughter, calamity, plague, pestilence," and is derived from the Hebrew word *nagaph*, meaning "to strike, smite." It does not necessarily refer to widespread disease, but is more often used to indicate great death in the context of judgment.

When we carelessly observe that thousands of people die in this or that *"plague,"* it is easy to make the mistake of wondering how this can be fair, for in each plague some die and others do not. The fact that the second census is taken immediately after this last plague speaks to the sovereign selection of God in exactly who would die in such a plague. The context suggests that this plague may have put to death all who remained alive from the fateful day of disobedience at the border of the Promised Land.

In Numbers 26 we see that in the second census the men of Israel have decreased by 1,820 even though children had been born those forty years.

All total, if you add up all the information the Bible gives us about the wilderness years, approximately 1,200,000 people died in those forty years.

📖 Look at Numbers 26:63–65. Who were left of the men who were numbered in the first census at Sinai?

_____

What do we learn about God from this?

_____

_____

We see here that none of the men who were numbered in the first census were to be found in the second census except Moses, Caleb, and Joshua. God has fulfilled his promise that the men would die in the wilderness. God always keeps His word. This speaks loudly of the tragedy of Israel's unwillingness to take God at His word forty years earlier.

In Numbers 27 we see Joshua commissioned before the congregation as Moses' replacement to lead them into the Promised Land. In preparation for the conquest of Canaan and the apportionment of the land, new leaders are identified for each of the twelve tribes. Once again, we see Caleb as the representative for the tribe of Judah (Numbers 34:18–19).

📖 Thinking through what you know of Caleb, how old do you think he is at this point?

_____

We know that thirty-eight years have passed. We know that at the time of the first census Caleb must have been at least twenty years old. That means that the youngest he could have been during the events recorded in Numbers 34 was fifty-eight years old. Actually he was probably much older than that, for at the first census and the selection of the twelve spies he had already achieved a place of prominence as the leader of his tribe. According to Joshua 14:7, he was forty years old when he spied out the land. Thus, he was seventy-eight when Joshua was commissioned as the new leader (Numbers 27). Humanly speaking, Caleb was well beyond the age for military service, but God had honored his faith, and here, at age seventy-eight, he prepares to lead his tribe into Canaan to fight for the new land.

> *Humanly speaking, Caleb was well beyond the age for military service, but God had honored his faith, and here, at age seventy-eight, he prepares to lead his tribe into Canaan to fight for the new land.*

Caleb **DAY FOUR**

THE CONQUEST OF CANAAN

Although as a leader of one of the twelve tribes Caleb would have been in the thick of each battle, we don't see him mentioned by name again until Joshua 14. As Joshua begins to divide the land, Caleb speaks up, reminding Joshua of what God had said forty-five years earlier.

In Deuteronomy 1:35–36, what did God promise Caleb at the beginning of the Wilderness journey?

_____

_____

"Caleb the son of Jephunneh . . . shall see it, and to him and to his sons I will give the land on which he has set foot, because he has followed the LORD fully." Although his age and faithfulness could have earned him an easier assignment, Caleb wanted what God intended for him. In Caleb we see a complete satisfaction with whatever the will of God provides.

📖 Read Joshua 14:6–12. What does Caleb say about his report of the land forty years earlier (v. 7)?

_____

How did Caleb follow the Lord (v. 8) and what did God promise him on that day (vv. 6 and 9)?

_____

_____

_____

To whom did Caleb give credit for being one of the only survivors in the wilderness (v. 10)? Who does Caleb credit for his ability to take that land (v. 12)?

_____

_____

How old was Caleb at this point (v. 10)?

_____

We see here that the report Caleb brought back when he first spied the land was simply *"as it was in* [his] *heart."* His heart was trusting in God. Verse 8 reports that Caleb followed the Lord fully. God promised Caleb the land on which he walked as an inheritance for him and his descendants forever. Even in verse 10 we see that Caleb gives credit where credit is due because his focus is on God and His promises (notice the phrase, *". . . just as He spoke"*). We also see here that Caleb is now eighty-five, but just as strong as he was when he first spied out the land and fully able for the war ahead.

📖 Read Joshua 14:12–14.

What was Caleb's request?

_____

_____

What was his attitude?

_____

_____

And how did Joshua respond?

_____

_____

Caleb asks for the hill country because it was what God had promised to him. It was certainly not the easiest conquest, for the Anakim lived there (descendants of the Nephilim—reputed to be giants along the lines of

> *"Caleb . . . shall see it, and to him and his sons I will give the land on which he has set foot, because he has followed the LORD fully."*
> Deuteronomy 1:36

Goliath). Yet Caleb trusted God's word to him. His attitude is not one of presumption. He uses the same words Jonathan would use against the Philistines in 1 Samuel 14:6—*"perhaps the Lord will be with me."* As a result, Joshua blesses him and gives him Hebron, for he *"followed the Lord fully."*

📖 Read Joshua 15:13–17. How did Caleb respond to Joshua's imparting of the inheritance (Joshua 14:13)?

_____

_____

_____

We see from Joshua 15 that Caleb was personally involved in the battles to possess the land, and the Lord gave him victory. Joshua 14:15 ends with a fitting evidence of God's reward for Caleb's faith and faithfulness—*"Then the land had rest from war."* It is significant that Hebron was the place where Abraham sojourned before and after his time in Egypt. It was there that Abraham built an altar and worshiped the Lord, and near there that Sarah was buried.

"Then the land had rest from war...." Joshua 14:15

Caleb DAY FIVE

FOR ME TO FOLLOW GOD

Caleb's testimony is a simple one—he trusted God. In his life we see the essence of what true faith is—taking God at His word: believing that what God says He will do, He does, that what He says will happen, will happen. That is what faith is, and that was consistently the mark of Caleb's life. If we are wise, we will learn what faith and faithfulness are all about.

📖 Read Numbers 13:2. What did God say about the land?

_____

_____

📖 Read Numbers 13:25–33. What is Caleb's personal choice concerning going into the land?

_____

_____

_____

📖 Read Numbers 14:1–10. Did he have any opposition?

_____

Describe everything that Caleb was up against by checking all that apply:

____ 10 men whose integrity he was calling into question
____ 1.2 million angry people screaming at him
____ his own question that he may have misunderstood God
____ 1.2 million fearful people ready to stone him
____ giants in the land

Humanly speaking, which choice would have been easier for Caleb to make?

    ___ to do as God instructed, despite the circumstances, and take the land

    ___ to go along with the other spies and gain approval in the people's eyes

    ___ to keep quiet and not "rock the boat" because it wasn't his problem

Why did he choose what he did (Numbers 13:2; Joshua 14:7–8)?

_____

_____

_____

_____

_____

Caleb took God at his word, even though it was the more difficult path, because he trusted that God's way was best. Caleb knew that when God said "I will give you the land" it was a done deal and their part was simply to follow.

APPLY What are some choices you are presently facing where faith and obedience are going to be more difficult than taking the easy way out?

_____

_____

_____

_____

_____

_____

APPLY Following God is a choice. He wants you to choose His way, trusting Him that it is best for you. So, are you willing to follow God fully and walk by faith even if it means life is harder because of it? Write out your choice to God.

_____

_____

_____

_____

_____

_____

_____

Following God is a choice. He wants you to choose His way, trusting Him that it is best for you.

Spend some time in prayer with the Lord right now.

Lord, forgive me for my distraction with the worries of this world. So often I trust my own understanding rather than Your sovereign sufficiency. Teach me Your Word, that I may learn to depend completely upon You. I would choose this day to follow You fully, with my whole heart to seek Your ways. No matter what circumstances may trouble me, no matter what hardships I may encounter, no matter what overwhelming opposition may confront me, my trust shall remain steadfastly in You. Lord, in my weakness, I cry out for your help to follow this choice. I believe; help my unbelief. In Jesus' name, Amen.

Write out your prayer. Remind yourself of His faithfulness to reveal Himself and His way to the seeking heart.

_____

_____

_____

_____

_____

_____

_____

_____

_____

_____

_____

Notes

Notes

Joshua

THE NECESSITY OF HUMILITY

*T*he life of Joshua is a picture of humility, a genuine humility marked by teachability, availability, obedience, and faithfulness. He experienced life as a faithful husband and father, as a humble servant of Moses, as a capable military commander, and as a teachable spiritual leader. In each of those areas he walked the path as a learner. He was not an instant success or perfect in every way, but he was a steady and faithful disciple of the Lord God of Israel. Joshua had a heart for God. He was marked by a teachable heart and mind and a willing spirit. He was an example to the people of Israel, and he serves as a model today for what it means to follow God. We can learn from Joshua at every point in his life—as a young man, as a growing leader, as commander over the people of God, and as the aged patriarch exhorting the people to *"serve the LORD."* In all of this he shows us the necessity of humility in following God and in leading others to follow Him.

> *Joshua was marked by a teachable heart and mind and a willing spirit.*

WHERE DOES HE FIT?

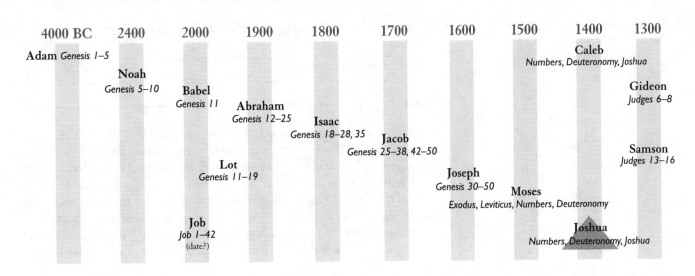

| 4000 BC | 2400 | 2000 | 1900 | 1800 | 1700 | 1600 | 1500 | 1400 | 1300 |

Adam *Genesis 1–5*

Noah *Genesis 5–10*

Babel *Genesis 11*

Abraham *Genesis 12–25*

Isaac *Genesis 18–28, 35*

Jacob *Genesis 25–38, 42–50*

Lot *Genesis 11–19*

Joseph *Genesis 30–50*

Moses *Exodus, Leviticus, Numbers, Deuteronomy*

Caleb *Numbers, Deuteronomy, Joshua*

Gideon *Judges 6–8*

Samson *Judges 13–16*

Job *Job 1–42* (date?)

Joshua *Numbers, Deuteronomy, Joshua*

MENTORED UNDER MOSES,
TAUGHT BY THE LORD

The first record of the life of Joshua is found in the book of Exodus. Exodus 1—3 tells us the story of the Israelites in Egyptian slavery. Joshua was born into that slavery. He was of the house of his father Nun, of the tribe of Ephraim. (For a chronology of the life of Joshua, see the **The Life of Joshua** chart at the end of this lesson.)

The first mention of Joshua is in Exodus 17, when Amalek attacked the weak rear ranks of Israel (see also Deuteronomy 25:17–19). At the age of fifty, Joshua was given the assignment of leading Israel into battle with Amalek. While Joshua led the battle at Rephidim, Moses, aided by Aaron and Hur, held up the staff of God, symbol of the presence and power of the Lord. Through this rod, the Lord had revealed Himself strong in Egypt and at the Red Sea, and now He again worked to show His power and the absolute necessity of dependence on Him. Because of that dependence, Joshua and his men prevailed. Joshua began to learn some valuable truths. Scripture shows that if we have a teachable heart we can learn much through the incidents of life.

📖 Read Exodus 17:8–16. What do you think Joshua learned in this battle?

_____

_____

_____

_____

What did God want recited to Joshua (v. 14)?

_____

_____

In verse 15, what did Moses call the altar?

_____

What truths was God trying to teach Joshua through this incident?

_____

_____

_____

Joshua was given the command to choose men and lead them in the fight against Amalek. It was a new responsibility and a new experience of learning the ways of God. He would have seen the necessity of dependence on the Lord represented in the staff of God. When the Lord called on Moses to write of this incident and of God's judgment of Amalek in a book and recite it to Joshua, it is evident that He wanted Joshua to have a clear understanding of the enemies of God and how to deal with them. The altar built there was named *"The LORD is My Banner."* The Lord was the standard under

Did You Know?
"THE LORD IS MY BANNER"

A banner was a sign, like a flag or a standard. It was a point of reference for the armies of Israel. A banner served as:

- A point of identity—each soldier knew where to turn to, who to follow, and which way to go.

- A point of unity—each man knew he was lined up and fighting together with fellow soldiers. The banner served as their rallying point.

- A point of victory—each soldier knew that the banner they fought under, the staff of God, was representative of the name, authority, and power of God. And it was He who was the true source of victory.

which true victory could be experienced. The staff served as a focal point of true worship and a visible reminder of the faithfulness of God to fulfill His promises to His people and to lead, guide, and protect them wherever they went.

In Exodus 24, we discover that Joshua served as Moses' personal assistant and servant. Under the guidance of Moses, who talked with God face to face as friend with friend, Joshua had the opportunity to learn much, if he would be available and teachable.

When God summoned Moses to Mt. Sinai to receive the law on stone tablets, Joshua went with him. Deuteronomy 9:9 tells us that during those forty days Moses did not eat or drink, implying that in the fullness of God's presence there was complete satisfaction and every need was met.

📖 Read Exodus 24:12–18. What do you think Joshua would have learned during those forty days?

_____

_____

_____

_____

During the unique events of those forty days, Joshua had to be impacted by the fiery appearance of the Lord on the mountain and the fact that Moses was there with the Lord and required nothing from Joshua, his personal assistant. Joshua had the opportunity to see once again, as he had in battle with Amalek, that the Lord is sufficient for every need and in every circumstance. He was being taught through a relationship God had put in His life. Through his relationship with Moses, Joshua had the opportunity to see what it meant to walk with God. God has given us instructions for life in His Word, as well as the example of men who followed Him. But He also puts people in our lives today that He can use to teach us.

 Where can you personally find others to learn from who are more spiritually mature than you are? (Circle all that are available to you.)

Church	Fellowship Groups
Sunday School Classes	Bible Studies
Accountability Groups	Christian Organizations
Bible School	Christian Friend
Parent	Other Family Members

Others _____

Have you taken advantage of any of these relationships to learn from others and allow God to work in your life as a result of them? If you have, how have they been valuable to you?

_____

_____

_____

_____

If you haven't taken advantage of these relationships, indicate which of the following best describes why.

____ I have never considered it very important.

____ I have prayed, and God has not yet brought such a person into my life.

____ I have spent my time learning from those who are considered successful by the world.

____ I have just moved to this area and have not settled in yet.

____ I can't find the time to devote to this type of relationship.

____ I have never been comfortable enough around "these types of people" to develop a close relationship.

____ Or is there another reason? _____

_____

One of the things that set Joshua apart was his teachable spirit. As He seeks to conform us to the image of Christ, God desires that we, too, first have a teachable, moldable spirit. We can be taught when we are hungry to learn.

📖 According to Exodus 33:7–11, what did Joshua do when Moses spoke with the Lord at the Tent of Meeting?

_____

_____

What does this tell you about Joshua?

_____

_____

_____

_____

Joshua was hungry to learn, to know the full meaning of following God.

At the tent of meeting outside the camp, Moses often met with the Lord. Joshua, Moses' servant, stayed in the tent of meeting after Moses returned to the camp. It is significant that Moses wrote this account found in Exodus. The attitude, heart, and action of Joshua in remaining in the tent of meeting made an impact on Moses. Joshua wasn't just "tagging along" on Moses' relationship with God; he was learning from Moses how to develop his own relationship with God. The Lord, as the Author of Scripture (2 Peter 1:21), made sure this characteristic of Joshua was recorded for us to read, meditate on, and apply to our lives. Joshua was hungry to learn, to know the full meaning of following God. This truth about the life of Joshua helps us see a crucial part of the making of a man of God and the equipping of a leader in the service of the Lord. Joshua deliberately made Himself available to the voice of God.

APPLY When was the last time you took some time apart for no other reason than to listen to God and allow Him to teach you?

_____

_____

_____

Time spent with God is never wasted. It is as vital to our spiritual health as food and water are to our physical well-being. Who better to learn from than the One Who knows *all* things? Think now about setting aside a regular time and place in your life to meet with God.

Joshua grew in his relationship to the Lord as the people of Israel drew nearer to the promised goal—life in the Promised Land. Two years after leaving Egypt, the Israelites came to Kadesh-Barnea in the southern part of Canaan. What had been promised to Abraham over four hundred years before, then to Isaac, Jacob, Joseph, Moses and the people of Israel, was about to become a reality, and Joshua was eager to enter into that promise. From Kadesh-Barnea the Lord wanted them to enter the land, but first they needed a view of the Promised Land.

The idea for spying out the land of Canaan came from the Lord. He instructed Moses to select a leader from each of the twelve tribes to go in and *"spy out the land of Canaan, which I am going to give to the sons of Israel"* (Numbers 13:2). Among the twelve chosen were Caleb and Joshua (Numbers 13:6, 8, 16). Here was the opportunity to be taught through "on-the-job training." This task was an opportunity to see first-hand the truthfulness, faithfulness, and trustworthiness of the Lord their God and, through that, to come to a deeper level of trust in God.

The twelve spies were given the task of viewing the land for forty days and then reporting on this land the Lord had promised them. When the men returned, all of them agreed that it was a land of plenty (Numbers 13:25–33). But ten of the twelve also said it was a land full of strong people and fortified cities. They said, *"We became like grasshoppers in our own sight, and so we were in their sight"* (13:33).

The report of the ten was marked by unbelief, emphasizing their view of the land, of the Canaanites, and of themselves, rather than a true view of God and His sure promises. The result was the spread of unbelief among the people. They did not listen to the Lord's voice but rather spurned Him, His name, and His honor. In essence, they rejected the land He was giving, so He let them have their way (Numbers 14:1–4, 22–35).

The report of Joshua and Caleb, on the other hand, was marked by faith. Their on-the-job training had succeeded. They did not test the Lord or grumble and complain, and they sought to focus the people on the good land and the ability of the Lord to give it to them as promised. They urged the people not to rebel against the Lord whose presence was promised and not to fear the Canaanites whose protection had been removed. The people spoke of stoning Joshua and Caleb, but the glory of the Lord appeared and silenced all opposition (Numbers 14:5–10).

The Lord was ready to start over with the family of Moses, but Moses interceded both for the sake of the people and of the honor and reputation of the Lord (Numbers 14:11–21). The Lord pardoned the people, but in His discipline sent them back into the Wilderness to wander and die. Of the men age twenty and over, only Joshua and Caleb would enter the promised land (14:22–30). The Lord said of Caleb, *"he has had a different spirit and has followed Me fully"* (14:24). That spirit was contagious to Joshua, if to no other, and both men were assured a place in the Promised Land. Joshua had begun to be the leader God wanted him to be. But first, he would have to wander in the Wilderness with the rest.

Word Study
JOSHUA'S NAME

Before he sent the spies into Canaan, Moses changed Joshua's name from **Hoshea** (Hebrew: *hoshea'*), which means "salvation" to **Joshua** (Hebrew: *yehoshua'*), meaning "Jehovah/Yaweh is salvation." (See Numbers 13:16.) The name Joshua is the Hebrew equivalent of the Greek word for **Jesus**.

AVAILABLE TO GOD, USEABLE AMONG MEN

As the people wandered in the Wilderness for the next thirty-eight years, the Lord continued to train Joshua for his role in conquering and settling the land of Canaan. Around 1406 BC, the Israelites came to the border of Canaan once again, this time on the east side of the Jordan River. The Lord told Moses his leadership of the people was about to end. It was time for Moses to hand the reins of leadership over to someone else—someone available to lead God's people God's way. In response, Moses prayed about a new leader.

📖 Read Numbers 27:12–18. Why do you think Moses would call the Lord, *"the God of the spirits of all flesh"*?

_____

_____

What do you think his reason was for using that particular name of God in this circumstance?

_____

_____

Moses knew that the Lord has an intimate knowledge of the thoughts and motives of every man. With that knowledge the Lord knew who was, first of all, spiritually fit to lead the congregation. The Lord knew who was available to Him from the heart and therefore useable among men. And God could reveal that to Moses.

What picture is given to reveal what the new leader should be (v. 17)?

_____

What qualities must a good shepherd possess?

_____

_____

_____

Moses prayed for a man who would be useable to God as a true shepherd of the people, who would know how to *"lead them out and bring them in."* The picture here is of a shepherd tenderly caring for his sheep in every detail—guiding them, providing for them, guarding them from harm, doing what is best for them. This was not just a job of general oversight. God needed someone who was available to do every task required.

The Lord named the new leader. What characteristic did the Lord focus on according to verse 18?

_____

> **Moses knew that leadership of the people of God must be by a man chosen of God, so Moses called on God.**

Why was this important?

_____

_____

_____

The Lord selected Joshua, *"a man in whom is the Spirit,"* as the man to lead Israel (27:18). Joshua had a personal relationship with the Lord. By His Spirit came the power and wisdom for daily life and leadership of the people of God. Because Joshua was available to the Lord personally, God could use him to lead the people.

📖 Read Deuteronomy 31:14–23. What were the two commands the Lord gave to Joshua as He commissioned him (v. 23)?

_____

_____

And the two promises?

_____

_____

The Lord gave Joshua two commands: **1)** be strong and **2)** be courageous. This pertained to his personal walk as well as his God-given assignment. The Lord also promised two things: **1)** Joshua would bring the people into the Promised Land and **2)** the Lord Himself would be present with Joshua. By God's power and presence Joshua would do what God wanted.

God wanted Joshua to be more than just a military commander. First and foremost, there had to be a personal relationship between Joshua and the Lord. The Lord met with him and spoke to him personally, and Joshua needed to be available to God for this relationship to continue. Then his task followed: to guide the people in following God with a whole heart before anything else. He needed to know the nature of the people he would lead and the Lord was faithful to tell Joshua exactly what they were like. The Lord had a plan, and He wanted Joshua to be fully prepared for the fulfillment of that plan.

Joshua was available *to* the Lord, *for* the task the Lord had, *with* the people God chose. It was important for the people to see Joshua as their new leader.

📖 Read Numbers 27:18–23. What did God command in verses 18–21?

_____

_____

_____

_____

What gave Joshua authority in the eyes of the people?

_____

_____

> **By God's Spirit in Joshua's life came the power and wisdom for daily life and leadership of the people of God.**

As outward preparation for leadership (in addition to the forty years Joshua had spent under the instruction and mentoring of Moses) Moses was told to lay his hand on Joshua. This was a sign of identification with Moses and his God-given authority, as well as a way to convey the passing of that authority to Joshua. The Lord also instructed Moses to *"give some of your authority"* to Joshua (NKJV). This was to be done before Eleazar the priest, representative of the holy standards of God, and before the congregation to publicly affirm God's choice of Joshua as the new leader.

How would Joshua know where to lead the people (v. 21)?

_____

_____

Did You Know?
URIM AND THUMMIM

The Hebrew words, *urim* and *thummim*, mean "lights" and "perfections." According to Exodus 28:30, these two objects were placed in the breastplate of the high priest ("the breastplate of judgment," i.e., of decision making). The high priest would wear them over his heart before the Lord continually, a constant sign of dependence on the Lord for guidance and wisdom in decisions and crises (Leviticus 8:8; Numbers 27:21; Deuteronomy 33:8).

Through the use of the Urim by Eleazar the priest, Joshua would know the will of the Lord and the direction to go. Not only would God guide Joshua directly, but Joshua had to be available for God to use others to guide him as well. Moses and Aaron had led the people for forty years. Now Joshua and Eleazar would lead the people.

According to Deuteronomy 34:9 Joshua was *"filled with the spirit of wisdom,"* and the people listened to him and followed his leadership. Moses laid his hands on Joshua because he was God's choice, and God chose him because Joshua was available to Him and therefore useable among men. The people honored that. And they followed what Moses had said in honoring Joshua as their new leader.

Soon after Joshua's commissioning by the Lord and by Moses, Moses died on Mount Nebo, in the area east of the Jordan River. It was now up to Joshua to follow God and lead the people into the land of Canaan, the land chosen for them and promised to them by their covenant-making and covenant-keeping Lord.

Joshua DAY THREE

JOSHUA: OBEDIENT FOLLOWER OF GOD AND LEADER OF THE PEOPLE OF GOD

Joshua now faced the land of Canaan without his mentor and spiritual father, Moses. The Lord, however, wanted Joshua to know that the source of victory and abundant life was not Moses or in Joshua himself. The victory would come from the Lord, as Joshua obeyed God's full direction. When we open the first pages of the book of Joshua, we find the Lord speaking very clearly and confidently concerning the task ahead. For Joshua to obey, he first had to hear the instructions of the Lord.

📖 Read Joshua 1:1–9. What does the Lord say about the land (vv. 2–4, 6)?

_____

_____

This was a specific place: the land God had promised. There was no other like it—the covenant-land of the covenant-God. And God specifically instructed Joshua on what land they were to take.

What does God say about the Law (vv. 7–8)?

_____

_____

_____

_____

The Law of the Lord God was a set of defining principles. The Law was given to this people to set them apart as the people of God. The people were told to carefully obey the Law and *"meditate on it day and night"* (v. 8). This obedience would ensure their success in all things.

And what does He say about Himself (vv. 5 and 9)?

_____

_____

_____

Here was a defining presence—the promised presence of the Lord God Himself. He promised to be with Joshua *"wherever you go."* God would not fail them.

What command does the Lord repeat three times to Joshua (vv. 6, 7, and 9)?

_____

_____

The Lord tells Joshua three times to *"be strong and courageous."* There were three reasons Joshua was able to obey this command: first, the promise of God (v. 6); second, obedience to the law of God (v. 7); and third, the presence of God Himself (v. 9). It all came down to God, even Joshua's obedience. And he had learned he could depend on God.

This was a defining point in time for Joshua. It was after the death of Moses—the leader of the people of Israel for over forty years was gone. It was now time for Joshua to be obedient in the role for which God had gifted, equipped, called, and commissioned him.

APPLY God never calls us to something for which He has not prepared us and through which He will not walk with us. Knowing this makes obedience easier. Have you ever been anxious about a task God has placed before you because you thought you weren't up to the challenge?

_____

_____

_____

_____

"Be strong and courageous! Do not tremble or be dismayed, for the LORD your God is with you wherever you go."
Joshua 1:9

What did you do?

_____

_____

_____

_____

Put Yourself In Their Shoes

SURRENDER TO THE LORD

Don't yield to the temptation to surrender to human weaknesses, physical frailties, or short-sighted, man-centered fears. Surrender to the Lord. In Him is no weakness of any kind.

Once we have heard the Lord, we may respond with a measure of doubt. We often react to challenges that seem beyond our abilities in a spirit of fear. In essence, the Lord was saying to Joshua, don't yield to the temptation to surrender to human weaknesses, physical frailties, or short-sighted, man-centered fears. Surrender to the Lord. In Him is no weakness of any kind. There is no danger in obeying Him; it is the safest place we can be. Fear the Lord, knowing that in fearing Him there is no need to fear anything else. The man who fails to surrender to the Lord will find himself surrendering to the many weaknesses of the flesh, his own and those of others. The man who fails to fear the Lord will be subject to a thousand lesser fears.

Joshua heard. Joshua surrendered. Then Joshua was ready to act. He faithfully obeyed and immediately began making preparations to cross the Jordan. He sent two spies to *"go, view the land, especially Jericho"* (2:1). The spies learned that *"surely the LORD has given all the land into our hands, and all the inhabitants of the land, moreover, have melted away before us"* (2:24). The people proceeded to the edge of the Jordan, where they made preparations to cross over.

Finally, after nearly forty years, they would have the chance to be obedient to God in taking the land He had promised them. Imagine their excitement! Children grew up in the wilderness hearing about the Promised Land of God. Mothers who had lived "out of a suitcase" for forty years could finally plan a home they didn't have to pack up. There must have been a temptation to fear as well—the ungodliness of the Canaanites, their wickedness and strength. But in those years Israel had learned to trust and obey God, to fear nothing beside Him. And they had a leader provided by Him in Joshua.

At this point it is important to understand why Joshua was commanded to go into Canaan, conquer the land, and destroy the inhabitants. There are two factors that enter into this equation. First, God had selected Abraham to be the father of a chosen people, and He had given them a chosen place to live—the land of Canaan (Genesis 15:1–21). And second, God saw the wickedness of the people of Canaan and in His holiness judged them and their sin.

📖 Read Leviticus 18:1–5 and 20:1–23. In your own words, what characterized the Canaanites?

_____

_____

_____

_____

_____

_____

How did God respond to the wickedness of the people of Canaan (v. 23)?

_____

_____

_____

_____

_____

_____

_____

Joshua knew why he had to be obedient in destroying the inhabitants of the land. The *"iniquity of the Amorite"* (see Genesis 15:16) was now full. These people had been given over four hundred years (since the time of Abraham) to acknowledge the true God and follow Him. They heard of His mighty deeds in Egypt forty years before Joshua came, and they still did not turn to God. Their idolatrous corruption and decay, as pictured in Leviticus 18 and 20 was abhorrent to God. The nations of Canaan brought judgment and the sentence of execution on themselves. God had a people whom He had chosen to walk in holiness before Him (Leviticus 20:24, 26) to possess this land and to carry out His judgment. (See Joshua 11:16–20 as well.)

Joshua knew that it was essential to follow all the Lord said. The past had shown him that trusting human reasoning and human abilities is foolishness. The way for God's plan to be accomplished in our lives is for us to depend on God to make it happen and follow Him. Joshua was willing and prepared to act on what God had said.

📖 Look at Joshua 3:5. How were the people to prepare for crossing the Jordan?

_____

_____

_____

> **The way for God's plan to be accomplished in our lives is for us to depend on God and follow Him.**

Joshua told the people to *"consecrate"* themselves. This involved being physically and ceremonially clean, an outward sign of an inner reality. The people too had to hear and surrender to the Word of the Lord. They had to be willing and prepared to obey. This they did.

All Israel obeyed God and crossed the Jordan miraculously on dry ground (3:6–17). In Joshua 4:21–24 we read the account of Joshua setting up a monument of twelve stones at Gilgal so that future generations would know of God's faithfulness and power in the miraculous crossings of both the Red Sea and the Jordan River. In the month Abib (Nisan) the children of Israel had crossed the Red Sea on dry ground. Forty years later in the same month, they crossed at the Jordan River. The purpose for both miracles was the same: *"that all the peoples of the earth may know that the hand of the LORD is mighty, so that you may fear the LORD your God forever"* (4:24). Joshua was faithful to follow and obey what the Lord had told him.

FOLLOWING GOD MEANS FAITHFULNESS TO GOD

Joshua chapter five tells the story of the circumcision of the sons of Israel born in the Wilderness. There at Gilgal after seeing the awesome power of their covenant-keeping God, they observed this covenant requirement. A covenant-land required a covenant-people. Then on the fourteenth of the month they observed the Passover, a remembrance of their deliverance from the land and the ways of Egypt. On the fifteenth *"they ate some of the produce of the land"* (5:11), and on the sixteenth, the manna ceased (5:12). Living in the land had begun. The faithfulness of God could be seen all around them. Now all that remained was to conquer the Canaanite cities and towns. How would they do that?

The first city they came to was Jericho, a city strategically located for trade and fortified with massive walls. There was no question that they would conquer the city (Joshua 2:24), but how would they do it? The Lord gave clear directions to Joshua, and Joshua continued to be faithful to follow God.

📖 Read Joshua 5:13—6:5. Who was the *"man"* (5:14)?

_____

What were the two key points in His message to Joshua (5:15; 6:2)?

_____

_____

_____

And how did Joshua respond (5:14–15)?

_____

_____

_____

With sword drawn, the Man stood as the Captain of the Army of the Lord, a manifestation of the Angel of the Lord, the pre-incarnate Christ. He made it clear to Joshua that He was there to fight on behalf of Joshua and the people of God and that Joshua was called to reverent worship (*"remove your sandals . . . , the place . . . is holy"*) like Moses at the burning bush when God was preparing to deliver Israel from Egypt (Exodus 3:1–10). Now the Lord was preparing to bring Israel in to fully possess the land of Canaan, and Joshua needed to know Who was in charge, to worship Him as Lord, and to submit to Him as commander. The covenant-Lord would bring His chosen covenant-people into His chosen covenant-land. Joshua did just as the Captain said. He bowed in reverence and removed his sandals. He was prepared to conquer the land.

The Lord gave Joshua clear directions on how to conquer Jericho. It would not be by man's strategies or ingenuity. It would be by the work of the Lord. They were to march around the city for six days, and on the seventh day

Did You Know?
MANNA

Two-and-a-half months after they left Egypt, God began to provide manna for the nation of Israel. The word *manna* simply means "what is it?" (Exodus 16:15). The manna resembled small round seeds. Its taste is described to have been like fresh oil and like wafers made with honey. Every morning, each person gathered enough manna for one day, except on the day before the Sabbath, when they gathered for two days. They did not gather on the Sabbath, but ate the extra manna they had gathered before the Sabbath. Any extra gathered any other day would spoil. The day after the Israelites began to eat the food of Canaan, provision of the manna stopped.

they were to march around the city seven times, blow the trumpets, shout, and go in to conquer the city. When they followed the Lord's directions, the city walls crumbled inward and the army of Israel marched in and captured the city with a great victory.

Joshua and the people rejoiced over the victory at Jericho, but there were some matters that had to be addressed. They began to realize the importance of taking God and His Word seriously—in every detail. In the next battle, Joshua sent a small force of soldiers to conquer the small town of Ai. The result was utter defeat and the death of thirty-six men. Why?

📖 Read Joshua 6:16–19. According to verse 17, what did it mean that Jericho was *"under the ban"*?

_____

_____

What would happen if they broke the ban (v. 18)?

_____

According to verse 19, what was the purpose for the ban?

_____

_____

_____

In Joshua 6:17, 19, Joshua made it clear that Jericho *"belongs to the LORD."* It was like the offering of firstfruits, a representation that in reality all belonged to God and all was a gift from Him (Leviticus 23:10). Here the giving of Jericho and its treasures to the Lord would acknowledge that fact. All the treasures were to be considered *"holy to the LORD"*—totally set apart to Him for His use and purposes. To dishonor this was to blatantly dishonor the LORD and His covenant, and to court disaster.

📖 Read Joshua 7:1–15. What did Achan do (v. 1)?

_____

_____

According to verses 2–5, what was the result?

_____

_____

How did Joshua respond (vv. 7–9)?

_____

_____

_____

In verses 10–15, God gave Joshua specific instructions for Israel's restoration. By obeying these instructions, Israel could once again experience God's

Did You Know?
THE WALLS OF JERICHO

Archaeological excavations have discovered that Jericho actually had two walls, about thirty feet high. The outer wall was six feet thick, and the inner twelve feet, with a twelve to fifteen foot space between them. The city itself was relatively small, and as it became crowded people built their houses between the walls. The excavated walls and city show signs of violent destruction.

Doctrine
FIRSTFRUITS

The firstfruits of the land were to be devoted wholly to the Lord as a mark of His ownership over all the land. Thus, Jericho was the firstfruits of the Promised Land, and the firstfruits of each harvest were offered to the Lord.

This concept continues in our lives today through a lifestyle of giving. The firstfruits of all we receive from God are offered to Him as a mark of His ownership over all we have. The principle applies not only to our possessions, but also to our time and our very lives.

presence and power. What was the essence of these instructions? Check all that apply.

___ The guilty person must stand before the children of Israel, confess, and return all stolen goods.
___ Destroy the stolen items.
___ Offer sacrifices to the Lord God.
___ Burn the one who was responsible for stealing.
___ Call the people to consecrate themselves.
___ Recite the Law continuously for seven days and seven nights.

Joshua 7:1 reveals that Achan broke the ban by stealing gold, silver, and precious fabric. As a result of Achan's sin, *"the anger of the LORD burned against the sons of Israel"* (v. 1), and the men of Israel were struck down when they attacked Ai. When Joshua and the leaders of the people fell before the ark of the covenant seeking the Lord, the Lord faithfully revealed that Israel had sinned and that sin had to be addressed. Faithfulness to God sometimes means dealing with the sins of others. Joshua had learned much from the Lord's dealings with His people and their sin when they had worshiped the golden calf, and when they had listened to and followed the unbelief of the ten spies. To ignore sin would be to face Canaan without the presence and power of the Lord. The Lord called Joshua to consecrate the people, and he called them to stand before the Lord clean and ready to obey Him. The next day the sin of Achan was revealed, and he and his family were judged (7:16–26). After that the nation conquered Ai with a great victory (8:1–29).

APPLY Are you harboring sin in *your* life right now?

_____

All sin affects our relationship with God, but it also affects our relationships with other people. If there is sin in your life, who do you think that sin might be affecting?

_____
_____
_____
_____
_____

Maybe you think it's not that big of a deal, or it doesn't affect anyone except you. But our sin does affect others around us—our family, our friends, our co-workers, our church. And like Achan, when we finally have to face the consequences of our sin, those around us often have to deal with those consequences as well.

Achan lost his own life and his family died with him (Joshua 7:24–25). Thirty-six men of Israel died in the failed attack on Ai. The consequences of Achan's theft were enormous. God puts a high price on sin. For Him, it is a matter of life and death, and He wants us to take it that seriously.

When we sin, what do we deserve?

_____for God's anger to burn against us
_____for others around us to be struck down and die
_____for God to remove His presence from us
_____for us to die

These are all things Achan faced because he yielded to temptation and did not deal with his sin. But God is not only a God of justice, He is also a God of mercy. And in His mercy, Jesus accepted the consequences upon Himself on our behalf. So, what does God then require of us to once again experience His presence and power?

Confession: agreeing with God that your sin is wrong and that you have no excuse.
Repenting: turning away from your own sinful way by choosing God and His way.
Yielding: submitting to His power to hold you to that choice, to direct and train you in His way.

 Think about your own life and the things you need to deal with God about. It is serious. Don't put it off.

Joshua then *"built an altar to the LORD, the God of Israel, in Mount Ebal"* (Joshua 8:30–35). There Joshua offered sacrifices and wrote the Law on stones and read it to all the people (compare Deuteronomy 27:1–26). The Lord knew His people. They needed to hear His Word often. The Lord had told Joshua to continually meditate on *"this book of the Law"* (Joshua 1:8), and Joshua gladly led the people to know and understand that book. The Lord wants us to follow Him in every detail of every day.

Joshua 9 illustrates the fact that we must be ever watchful. The Gibeonites (Hivites) deceived the Israelites into making a covenant with them. The Israelites depended on their own understanding and *"did not ask for the counsel* [literally, mouth] *of the LORD"* (9:14). They failed to seek what the Lord had to say before they acted, showing a lack of faithfulness. As a result, they had to deal with their own sin and its consequences. Joshua and the Israelites were required by covenant to protect them. The Lord used even this to bring His judgment on certain Canaanite peoples in the territory from Gibeon to Makkedah (Joshua 10:1–28).

Joshua 10 and 11 records the victories of Joshua over a seven-year period (1405–1398 BC). (See the **The Life of Joshua** chart.) When he obeyed the Word of the Lord he experienced victory. Then *"the land had rest from war"* (11:23), and Joshua and Eleazar divided the land among the tribes as the Lord directed (Numbers 34:16–17; Joshua 19:51).

Joshua 24:1–15 records Joshua's final message, at the age of 110, to all the tribes meeting at Shechem. He recounted the history of Israel and the faithfulness of God and then in verse 14 exhorted them to be faithful. We see in his last days Joshua made it clear that **faithfulness is a choice.**

Read Joshua 24:1–18. What four things does Joshua tell them (v. 14)?

_____

_____

_____

Did You Know
**"THE BOOK OF
THE LAW"**

For the Hebrews, "the book of the Law" included:

Genesis

Exodus

Leviticus

Numbers

Deuteronomy

Despite what they may decide, what does Joshua say he will do (v. 15)?

_____

_____

_____

What choice did they make (vv. 16–18)?

_____

_____

_____

Joshua focused the people's attention on the choice to fear (reverence) and serve the Lord only. The Lord had been faithful to them as their covenant-keeping God. They should be faithful to Him as His covenant-people. Joshua presented the people with the choice of following God or serving other gods. *"But,"* he tells them, *"as for me and my house, we will serve the Lord."* The people responded that they, too, would serve the Lord (vv. 16–24). So, Joshua led them in renewing their covenant with the Lord. He set up a memorial stone at Shechem as a continual reminder to the people of their relationship to the Lord and a witness to their vow.

"After these things . . . Joshua the son of Nun, the servant of the LORD, died" at the age of 110, a testimony of a faithful man, available to the Lord, and marked by humility and a teachable spirit.

Joshua

FOR ME TO FOLLOW GOD

Joshua's life is a valuable example of the necessity of humility. God did not force Joshua into a position of leadership. Joshua was teachable and available: available for however God wanted to use him, and teachable, realizing that in whatever God wanted him to do, God would teach him. God was faithful to teach and guide Joshua, and Joshua was faithful to listen, learn, and obey. Joshua knew that his leadership was worthless unless he was following God.

 What characteristics have you observed in Joshua's life that made him a follower of God, and thus, a successful leader of the people? Look at the references below and place a check mark in the appropriate box(es) which best reveal the humility evident in Joshua's life:

Exodus 24:12–18
• Joshua was ready to go when Moses asked (v.13).
• Joshua went with Moses (v. 13).
• Moses knew that Joshua would return with him (v. 14).

Exodus 33:7–11
• Joshua would not depart from the tent after Moses left (v. 11).

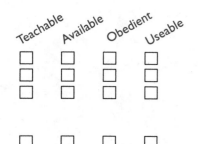

Numbers 14:6–10

- Joshua tore his clothes when he heard the people's response (v. 6).
- Joshua reminded the people of God's promise regarding the land (v. 7).
- Joshua recognized God's ultimate control over him and the people (v. 8).
- He reminded the people that God could take them into the land (v. 8).
- He reminds the people to not rebel against the Lord (v.9).
- Joshua tells them not to fear the people (v. 9).
- He tells them that all of this is possible because the Lord is with them (v. 9).

Numbers 27:15–23

Joshua is described as a man . . . (v. 17)
- who will go out and come in before them.
- who will lead them out and bring them in.
- God said that Joshua was a man in whom the Spirit lived (v. 18).
- Joshua was given authority over the people (v. 21)

Joshua 5:13—6:7

- Joshua fell on his face and bowed down before the captain of the host of the Lord (v. 14).
- Joshua asked him, *what has my lord to say to his servant?* (v. 14).
- The angel told him to remove his sandals; he did (v. 15).
- The Lord told Joshua how to conquer Jericho; Joshua did just as the Lord commanded him (vv. 1–7).

Many of us might look at Joshua's position of leadership and think it has little relevance to our own lives. But godly leadership involves much more than a position. We are all, consciously or not, leading someone.

APPLY Who in *your* life respects you and follows your lead? In other words, who do you influence (Check all that apply)?

___Employees
___Your spouse
___Acquaintances at church
___Students
___Children & teenagers you're around
___Co-workers
___Teammates

___Your children
___Friends
___Neighbors
___Your pastor
___Brothers and sisters
___Relatives
___Roommate

Your life influences many people every day. In which direction are you leading them? (Place an "x" in the appropriate location on the line below.)

Away from God ◄─────────────► **Closer to God**

No matter who you are and what you do, you are influencing other people with your life. The only way you can be sure of leading them in the right direction is if your focus is on following God and becoming closer to Him.

We saw certain characteristics in Joshua's life that made him a good follower of God. How much do these same characteristics show up in your life? Look at the areas of your life listed in the left hand column in the chart on the next page. Briefly describe some ways that the godly characteristics, listed across the top of the chart, are seen in your life.

	Teachable	Available	Obedient	Faithful
With God				
At Home				
At Work				
At Church				
With Friends				

How are these characteristics developed in your life?

✓ By humbling yourself under the hand of God—to be taught by Him in the incidents and relationships of life.

✓ By consistently spending time with Him in His Word, learning His will and His ways.

✓ By becoming open and transparent before God in prayer—available for whatever He wants.

Spend some time in prayer with the Lord right now.

Lord, forgive me for being so easily distracted from following You. Too often, everything else comes first. Make me more aware of those You have brought into my life to teach me, and help me to humble myself that I may learn from them. I am willing to do whatever tasks You place before me. Lead me in the life You would have me live. I will be satisfied with any service as long as it is of use to You. Only You know the true thoughts and motives of my heart—teach my heart obedience to Your Spirit. Help me to faithfully follow You so that I may be strong and courageous in all things, living in complete dependence on Your faithfulness. And may all who look to me see only You. In Jesus' name, Amen.

Write out your prayer to God asking Him to show you how to walk in humility before Him.

_____

_____

_____

_____

_____

_____

_____

_____

_____

A Look at Joshua's Life

DATE	EVENTS	SCRIPTURE
ca. 1496/95 BC	Joshua was born to the family of Nun, the tribe of Ephraim, in slavery with the people of God in Egypt. He was given the name Hoshea, which means "salvation."	Ex. 1 Ex. 3:7–10 Num. 13:16
1st Month, Abib (March/April) 1446/1445 BC	Led by Moses and Aaron, Joshua and the people made their Exodus from Egypt and began the Wilderness Journey to Mount Sinai.	Ex. 12:31–51; 13:17–22; 14—16 1 Kgs. 6:1
2nd Month, Iyyar 1445 BC	The people camped at Rephidim, and the Lord provided water from the Rock.	Ex. 17:1–7
2nd Month, Iyyar 1445 BC	At Rephidim, Moses appointed Joshua to lead Israel in the battle with Amalek. Joshua was victorious as Aaron and Hur held up the hands of Moses as he held the staff of God.	Ex. 17:8–16
3rd Month, Sivan (May/June) 1445 BC	Joshua served as Moses' servant and went up with Moses as he ascended on the mountain of God to receive the Law the first time. Moses was on the mountain for 40 days and nights receiving the Law. Joshua was nearby.	Ex. 24:13–18; 25—32:16
	Joshua heard the uproar of the camp of the Israelites and thought it was the sound of war, but it was the sound of idolatrous singing.	Ex. 32:17–19
	At the tent of meeting outside the camp, Moses often met with the Lord face to face as friend to friend. Joshua often stayed in the tent of meeting after Moses returned to the camp.	Ex. 33:7–11 [Note verse 11]
	Moses returned to the mountain for a second 40 days.	Ex. 34:1–29
1444 BC	On the way from Sinai to Kedesh the people complained of having only manna and no meat. The Lord instructed Moses to gather 70 elders and await the meat the Lord would send. At this time the Spirit of the Lord came upon the 70, and they prophesied. Joshua was concerned that they should stop prophesying. Moses corrected his concern.	Numbers 11:1–29 [Note verse 28]
ca. 1443 BC	Joshua's name was changed by Moses from Hoshea ["Salvation"] to Joshua ["Jehovah/Yahweh is Salvation].	Num. 13:8, 16
ca. 1443 BC for 40 days	Joshua served as one of the 12 spies sent from Kadesh-Barnea to spy out the land of Canaan for forty days and forty nights and report to the people.	Num. 13:1–3; 8, 17–33; 14:6–10
	Joshua and Caleb reported on the goodness of the land and called the people to trust and obey the Lord in going to conquer the land. All the others disbelieved.	Num. 14:6–10; Deut. 1:26–33
	Only Joshua and Caleb would be allowed to go into the land of Canaan, "for they have followed the Lord fully" (32:12). Joshua would lead them into the land of Canaan (1:38). All the others age 20 and older would die in the wilderness.	Num. 14:20–38 26:65; 32:11–12
1443–1405 BC	Joshua experienced the wilderness wanderings with the Israelites for 38 years. (Two years in the wilderness from Egypt to Mount Sinai to Kadesh-Barnea, plus 38 years wandering equals 40 years in the wilderness.)	Num. 4:11–45; 33; Deut. 2:7; 8:2–5; 29:5–9
1406–1405 BC	In Moses' last message, he spoke of Joshua as the leader who would take the people into the land. He charged him to be strong and courageous and assured him of the presence of the Lord.	Deut. 31:1–8 [Note vv. 3, 7, 8]
1406–1405 BC	The Lord met with Joshua and Moses at the tent of meeting and the Lord commissioned Joshua as leader of the people.	Deut. 31:14–15, 23
	The Lord spoke to Moses and Joshua about the coming unfaithfulness of the people in following foreign gods.	Deut. 31: 16–22
	The Lord instructed both Moses and Joshua to "write this song" [plural verb].	Deut. 31:30; 32:1–44
	Moses (with Eleazar the priest) commissioned Joshua as the leader of the congregation.	Num. 27:15–23; Deut. 31:23
	Moses gave command to Eleazar and Joshua concerning the participation of Reuben, Gad, and Manasseh in conquering the land [note verse 28]. Elsewhere, he encouraged Joshua that the Lord would give them victory.	Num. 32:20–28; 29—32; Deut. 3:21–22
	Near Beth-peor, the Lord instructed Moses to charge Joshua as the leader of the people of God and to encourage and strengthen him.	Deut. 3:23–29
	The Lord instructed Moses to appoint Eleazar and Joshua as the men who would apportion the land of Canaan to the tribes.	Num. 34:16–17

DATE	EVENTS	SCRIPTURE
	Joshua was present with Moses when he spoke the words of his Song	Deut. 31:30; 32:1–47
	Joshua was filled with the spirit of wisdom, and the people listened to him and followed him.	Deut. 34:9
	The Lord exhorted Joshua to be strong and courageous as the new leader of the children of Israel.	Josh. 1:1–9
	Joshua began leading the children of Israel in preparation for crossing the Jordan and conquering the land of Canaan.	Josh. 1:10–18
	Joshua sent two spies into Jericho.	Josh. 2:1–24
10th Day of the Month of Abib (March/April), 1405 BC	Joshua led the people from Shittim to the Jordan River, exhorted the people to consecrate themselves, and led them across the Jordan past the ark of the covenant, which was stationed in the middle and upheld on the shoulders of the priests.	Josh. 3:1–17
	Joshua brought the tabernacle into the land of Canaan.	Acts 7:45
	Joshua led the people to Gilgal where they set up twelve memorial stones taken from the Jordan. The Lord exalted Joshua in the sight of the people.	Josh. 4:1–24
Month of Abib 1405 BC	At Gilgal, Joshua led the people in circumcising all the sons of Israel who were born in the wilderness. They observed the Passover on the 14th of the month.	Josh. 5:1–12
Abib 15 & 16 1405 BC	The people ate the produce of the land on the 15th, and the manna ceased on the 16th day.	Josh. 5:11–12
	Joshua was met by the captain of the host of the Lord.	Josh. 5:13–15
7 days, 1405 BC	Joshua led the children of Israel in marching around the city of Jericho for seven days and then in capturing the city.	Josh. 6:1–27
7 days, 1405 BC	Joshua pronounced judgment on any who would rebuild Jericho. This prophecy was fulfilled in the life of Hiel of Bethel during the reign of King Ahab (ca. 874–853 BC).	Josh. 6:26; Fulfilled in 1 Kgs. 16:34
	Joshua dealt with the defeat at Ai and the sin of Achan. Then the Israelites captured Ai.	Josh. 7:1–26; 8:1–29
	Joshua built an altar on Mount Ebal, offered sacrifices, and wrote the Law on stones in obedience to Moses' command	Josh. 8:30–35 Deut. 27:1–26
	Joshua led the people in establishing a covenant with the Gibeonites without the counsel of the Lord.	Josh. 9:1–27
	In defense of the Gibeonites, Joshua fought the five Amorite kings (of Jerusalem, Hebron, Jarmuth, Lachish, and Eglon) and defeated them and their armies on the day the sun stood still.	Josh. 10:1–27
	Joshua conquered and destroyed the people of Makkedah, Libnah, Lachish, Gezer, Eglon, Hebron, and Debir—all the area from Kadesh-Barnea to Gaza and Goshen to Gibeon.	Josh. 10:28–43
	Joshua defeated the kings and armies of Hazor, Madon, Shimron, Achshaph, the northern mountain kings, Meggido, those of the plain of Chinneroth (Galilee), Dor, and Mizpah.	Josh. 11:1–15 See also 12:7–24.
1405–1398 BC	Summary of Conquests: Conquests in the South, Central, and the North, plus the 31 kings conquered west of the Jordan. [Chronology based on Joshua 14:7–10. Caleb's age at Kadesh-Barnea (40), at which point they had wandered already two years since the Exodus, plus 38 years of wilderness wanderings, plus 7 years of battles equals 85, the age of Caleb when he was given Hebron as an inheritance.]	Josh. 11:16–23; 12:7–24; [14:7–10]
ca. 1395 BC	The Lord recounted the land yet unconquered left to the tribes to conquer and commanded Joshua to divide the lands to the tribes by lot as their inheritance.	Josh. 13:1–33; 14:1—19:48, 51
	Joshua was given the city of Timnath-serah in the mountains of Ephraim.	Josh. 19:49–50
	Joshua appointed 6 cities of refuge: Kedesh, Shechem, Hebron, Bezer, Ramoth in Gilead, Golan.	Josh. 20:1–9
	Joshua and the leaders gave 48 cities to the Levites among the various tribal allotments.	Josh. 21:1–42

DATE	EVENTS	SCRIPTURE
	Under the leadership of Joshua, the people celebrated the Feast of Booths/Tabernacles.	Neh. 8:17
ca. 1385 BC	Joshua spoke to the tribes east of the Jordan—the tribes of Reuben, Gad, and the half-tribe of Manasseh. He commended their faithfulness to help the tribes west of the Jordan and exhorted them to keep the Law of the Lord.	Josh. 22:1–6
	Joshua gave his message to the tribes west of the Jordan exhorting them to remain faithful to the Lord and His Law.	Josh. 23:1–16
	At Shechem, Joshua gave his final message to all the tribes and led the people in renewing their covenant to follow the Lord and serve Him only.	Josh. 24:1–28; Judg. 2:6–7
	Under the hand of God, Joshua left certain nations in the land at the time of his death.	Judg. 2:21–23
ca. 1385-1383 BC	Joshua died and was buried in Timnath-Serah in the hills of Ephraim on the north side of Mount Gaash.	Josh. 24:29 Judg. 2:8–9

Notes

Gideon

LITTLE IS MUCH WHEN GOD IS IN IT

The age of Gideon was an era of judgment. Israel had turned from their Creator to gods of man's own creation. As a result, they spent seven years under the heavy hand of God's discipline. The instrument of Jehovah's chastisement was the Midianites. As the locusts to whom they are compared, these wandering Bedouins from Arabia would swoop down on Israel at the time of harvest in numbers too great to count, leaving behind no food for either men or cattle. Impoverished Israel would creep forth from their dens and caves to once again sow the land, but their harvest hopes would be dashed as another raid would plunder them afresh.

By God's design, their afflictions made them weary of their impotent idols, and drove them back to their first love, where the Lord waited to welcome His prodigal people home. It is at this juncture that Gideon arrives on the scene. He is a remarkably unremarkable man. Perhaps Gideon's greatest attribute is his smallness. God delights in using small men with big hearts so that all of the glory returns to Him where it belongs. At this dark time in Israel's history, Gideon is a torch light of trust in God's power to deliver and a reminder of God's covenant love for His people.

God delights in using small men with big hearts so that all of the glory returns to Him— where it belongs.

WHERE DOES HE FIT?

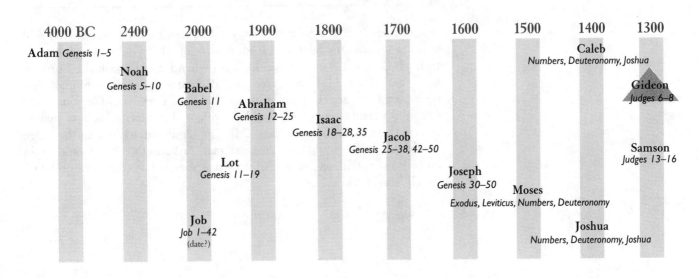

GOD TROUBLES GIDEON

The most important thing to realize as we study Gideon is that he did not seek out God. God sought out Gideon. In His grace, God chose a man that He could use to deliver Israel. We see this pattern repeated over and over during the period of the Judges. Israel would stray, and God would use other nations to chastise Israel and bring them to their senses. Then God would raise up a person to deliver them.

As one studies the book of Judges, it is important to remember that it was not written in a strictly chronological fashion. The first two chapters and the first six verses of chapter three give a political (chapter 1) and spiritual (2:1–3:6) background of the period. Then in 3:6 we begin to see the major judges laid out in a sequential manner—Othniel, Ehud, Deborah and Barak, Gideon (chapters 3–8), and then the seven overlapping judges (chapters 10–16). The last five chapters give a concluding overview of the apostasy of this period, but overlap chronologically with some of the previous chapters.

The term "judges" is from the Hebrew word, *shophetim*. Its root means "to put right, and so to rule," which is exactly what the judges did during this period. The period of the Judges is a sub-period at the end of the age of the Patriarchs, covering the turbulent era from about 1380 BC to about 1050 BC, and bridging the conquest of Canaan to the establishment of a monarchy. The last judge, Samuel, who also served somewhat as a prophet, provides a transition into this new period in Israel's history, the period of the Kings. We want to begin our consideration of Gideon by setting a context of the period in which he lived and how God was working among His people.

📖 Read Judges 2:1—3:6. There is a cycle of events during the period of the Judges. Look particularly at chapter 2, verses 11–23, and identify the four main elements that make up this cycle.

1) _____

2) _____

3) _____

4) _____

Judges 2:11–23 lays out for us a spiritual pattern that is repeated over and over throughout the book and is illustrative of what God was trying to do through Gideon. The cycle would begin when Israel forsook the Lord for other gods (2:11–13). Then God would chasten Israel by sending other nations against them to plunder them (2:14–15). They would cry out to the Lord (2:18), and God's grace would be evidenced by His raising up a man to deliver them from their enemies (2:16–18). Unfortunately, when the judge would die, Israel would again forsake the Lord and the cycle would begin all over again. Gideon was one of these deliverers whom the Lord raised up to call Israel back to Himself.

Gideon did not seek out God. God sought out Gideon.

What was going on in the particular time that Gideon was called out by the Lord?

📖 Read Judges 6:1–10. Why did the Lord give Israel into the hands of the Midianites for seven years?

_____

_____

What did the Midianites do to Israel that brought them *"very low"* (vv. 2–6)?

_____

_____

_____

_____

_____

What did the Israelites do after they had been brought low (v. 6)? How did the Lord respond (vv. 7–8)?

_____

_____

_____

Summarize what the Lord said to Israel through the prophet (vv. 8–10).

_____

_____

_____

_____

Verse 1 states emphatically that Israel *"did what was evil in the sight of the Lord,"* and as a result God gave them into the hands of Midian for seven years. It was so bad that many had to flee from their homes to live in caves. Whatever Israel would plant, Midian would destroy. Whatever livestock God's people possessed, the Midianites would steal and plunder.

But it is not until verses 8–10 that we begin to see the details of the evil Israel had done. They had forsaken the Lord and worshiped the gods of the Amorites who lived in the land. Their primary sin, other than that of idolatry, was one of forgetfulness—forgetting all that God had done for their parents. But even in all of this there is a reminder of grace, for God sends a prophet to them in answer to their cry, and then He raises up a deliverer. We are first introduced to Gideon when the angel of the Lord paid him a visit.

📖 Read Judges 6:11. What was Gideon doing when the angel of the Lord appeared to him, and why was he doing it?

_____

_____

_____

Did You Know?
THE MIDIANITES

The Midianites were probably the descendants of Midian, Abraham's fourth son by his second wife, Keturah. In the time of Joseph, they are closely associated with the Ishmaelites and had probably intermarried with them. Moses married the daughter of Jethro, the priest of Midian whose flocks he tended (Exodus 3:1). By the time Gideon encountered them, they had apparently become the first to domesticate and use the camel on a large scale. This would have given them the increased mobility in the desert to effectively raid the Israelites each harvest.

The text tells us that Gideon was *"beating out wheat in the wine press."* To make the fresh wheat into something useable, it first had to be beaten to knock the useless outer husks loose. Normally this activity would be performed on a threshing floor in an open area where the grain could be thrown into the air and the breeze would be allowed to blow the chaff (loose husks) away, leaving only the edible grain to fall to the ground. Instead, Gideon is performing this task out of sight in the wine press as an act of desperation, in fear that the Midianites would see and come to steal even the smallest amount of grain that could be threshed in this way. The *"angel of the LORD"* here is considered by most theologians to be a "theophany"—a pre-incarnate appearance of the Lord Jesus Christ.

📖 Read Judges 6:12–16. How does the angel of the Lord greet Gideon (v. 12)? How does Gideon respond (v. 13)?

_____

_____

_____

What is the Lord's answer to him, and what is Gideon's excuse (vv.14, 15)?

_____

_____

_____

_____

The angel of the Lord came to Gideon saying, *"The LORD is with you, O valiant warrior."* It is ironic that God should address Gideon so when he is hiding in the wine press. Gideon responds, "If God is with us, why is this happening? Where are the miracles of God?" The Lord basically says, "I'm looking at the deliverer." He makes it clear that Gideon is to be God's instrument of deliverance. Notice how insignificant Gideon seems: his family is the least of the small tribe of Manasseh. (This tribe was initially a "half-tribe," since Manasseh was one of the two sons of Joseph.) Not only is Gideon's family small, but Gideon is the youngest of his family.

Why do you think God would have chosen Gideon as the deliverer of Israel, when he was the youngest member in the seemingly insignificant family of Manasseh?

_____

_____

_____

God delights in using the small and young so He gets the greater glory.

📖 Read 1 Corinthians 1:26–29. What does this tell you about God's way of working in the world?

_____

_____

Gideon, in his desire to be certain of God's message, asks for a sign of God's favor (Judges 6:17–18), and with God's reassurance he builds an altar to the Lord and worships God. The angel of the Lord touched his offering with the end of His staff and fire sprang up from the rock and consumed the offering. Then the angel of the Lord vanished.

This idea of fire consuming an offering was evidence of God's acceptance of Gideon's offering and is reminiscent of the same miracle occurring at the inauguration of the priestly service with Moses and Aaron (Leviticus 9:24). This was God's sign to Gideon to reassure him that he had in fact been called by the Lord to a divine task. Having seen Gideon's smallness we can understand his hesitancy, and what a joy it is to be reminded that the Lord is patient with our doubts and faithfully communicates His will to us in a way we can understand.

GOD TESTS GIDEON

God had some eternally significant tasks for Gideon to do. Those tasks would require faith, availability, and the choice to take God at His word. We have seen God's patience with Gideon's doubts, but now we will also see that after answering those doubts, God expected Gideon to be willing to step out in obedience. It is significant that verse 25 begins, *"Now the same night. . . ."* God wasted no time in giving an assignment to Gideon. Ultimately God would use Gideon to "take on" the Midianites, but first Gideon had to "take on" the Israelites. Remember, the Midianites weren't the real problem—Israel was. It was Israel's forsaking of the Lord and their following other gods which had gotten them into their latest crisis. Before the Midianites were confronted, God wanted to confront the idols Israel had taken up. In Judges chapter 6, we see Gideon "step up to the plate" and embrace the task God had placed before him.

📖 Read Judges 6:25–27. What did God call Gideon to do?

_____

_____

_____

When did Gideon fulfill that task (v. 27)?

_____

_____

Why did he wait until it was night (v. 27)?

_____

_____

God called Gideon to tear down the altar of Baal which belonged to his father, and to cut down the Asherah (a wooden symbol of a female deity), building an altar to the Lord in its place. God is asking Gideon to take a stand; but more than that, God is asking Gideon to draw a line in his own heart. In this encounter we see a beautiful picture of repentance—Gideon repenting on behalf of himself, his family and his nation of worshiping other gods and returning to the worship of the one true God. Even though Gideon was not very courageous in his stand (for out of fear he performed the task at night) he does obey.

> **The Lord is patient with our doubts and faithfully communicates His will to us in a way we can understand.**

🖊 ***Did You Know?***
(?) **BAAL**

Baal was the son of El, the chief Canaanite deity. He was the farm god who reigned over crops and herds. The worship of Baal was characterized by revelry and licentiousness. Rites of worship were often held outdoors and included animal sacrifices, ritualistic meals, and immoral dances.

📖 According to Judges 6:28–30, how do God's chosen people, the Israelites, respond when they learn of the desecrated altar of Baal?

_____

_____

_____

The people were angered upon seeing their destroyed altar to Baal, and their first question was *"Who did this thing?"* Upon searching and discovering that Gideon was responsible, they went to Joash, the patriarch of the family, and demanded Gideon be brought out and put to death as punishment. Now, it is important to remember that the Israelites cried out to the Lord back in verse 7, yet here we see them trying to defend their pagan gods. So deep was their commitment to idolatry that they wanted to kill Gideon. We must never make the mistake of thinking that just because we have cried out to God and He has answered us, that He approves of all that is in our lives. God is faithful to us even when we are unfaithful to Him, but He does not ignore the sin in our lives.

📖 Read Judges 6:31–32. In Joash's defense of his son's actions, what does he reveal of his own belief in Baal?

_____

_____

_____

Gideon's father exhibited his wisdom with his quick and prudent answer to the mob. By asking, *"Will you contend for Baal?"* he backs the angry crowd down and in a sense, paints them into a corner. He is calling into question the power of the god they have been worshiping. If they maintained the necessity of revenge, by their actions they said that Baal was impotent and powerless. The other side of the coin (which the crowd obviously didn't think of) is that if they left revenge to Baal and nothing happened, this too would show that he was impotent and powerless. Joash's quick thinking (perhaps better recognized as God's wisdom given in the moment of need) insured that nothing further would be done to Gideon. In fact, out of this, Gideon was given a new name, *"Jerubbaal,"* which means *"Let Baal contend against him."*

To appreciate what God had done through Gideon, it is important to understand where the altar of Baal and the Asherah came from and God's perspective on them.

📖 Read Deuteronomy 7:1–6. What does God command the people concerning altars to other gods (v. 5)?

_____

_____

_____

Why are they to do this (v. 6)?

_____

_____

> **God is faithful to us even when we are unfaithful to Him, but He does not ignore the sin in our lives.**

In the book of Deuteronomy, Moses reviewed the instructions of God to prepare the people for entering the promised land. In these verses we get some idea how Israel entered into the worship of Baal. God had warned them to stay separate from the nations in the land. The implication of verse 3 is that Israel had intermarried with the inhabitants of the land and, through that, had been lured into their pagan forms of worship. How interesting that in verse 5 we see a specific instruction to *"tear down"* the pagan altars and destroy everything associated with that kind of worship. One cannot walk in the path of the world and remain unstained by it. God communicates His purpose for calling out Israel in verse 6—they are to be *"a holy people to the LORD. . . ."* What a sad contrast that instead of obeying the Lord and tearing down those pagan altars, the people of Israel wanted to kill Gideon for doing so.

The most important thing to recognize from today's study is that God placed a test before Gideon, and he passed this test with flying colors. It was a call for him to do what should have been done long before by the leaders of Israel. Yet it is this small man, Gideon, who finally obeys. All through Israel's history, God has looked not for men of outstanding ability, but for men with a willingness to trust and obey. Gideon is not a testimony of an unshakable faith, but rather of a very shaky faith placed in an unshakable God.

> **God looks not for men of outstanding ability, but for men with a willingness to trust and obey.**

GOD TOLERATES GIDEON

Perhaps there is no single event in Gideon's life for which he is more remembered than his unique method of determining God's will. When the second task is placed before him (to lead Israel into battle against the Midianites and the Amalekites), Gideon asks for further proof of God's call. Twice he asks for a sign from God to prove that God is indeed going to do what He says. What speaks most loudly in the incident of Gideon's fleece is not the method for determining God's will, but the tolerance of God for the method. We see from this very human incident that God is patient with our mortal uncertainties. The Psalmist wrote, *"He is mindful that we are but dust"* (Psalm 103:14).

📖 Read Judges 6:33–35. How did God prepare Gideon for what He was about to do (delivering Israel) through him (v. 34)?

_____

_____

_____

_____

> **What speaks loudest in the incident of the fleece is God's tolerance of Gideon's requests.**

The Midianites and Amalekites (those fierce pagan warriors who attacked Israel from the rear in the wilderness, killing the children and the aged) were making preparations to attack Israel. Battle was imminent. At this point, the Spirit of the Lord came upon Gideon, and he sounded a call gathering an army to do battle. In fact, the literal wording in verse 34 is that the Spirit *clothed* Gideon. In other words, the Spirit covered Gideon like a garment. God desires people who will allow Him to fill them and accomplish His work through them. The idea of the Spirit clothing Gideon not only communicates

God desires people who will allow Him to fill them and accomplish His work through them.

God's choice of Gideon, but Gideon's submission to that choice. Gideon's fearful obedience to God's call becomes a rallying point for Israel. In addition to the Abiezrites (the sub-tribe to which Gideon belonged), all of the tribe of Manasseh is represented as well as three other tribes of Israel (Asher, Zebulun, and Naphtali).

In considering the phrase, *"the Spirit of the LORD came upon Gideon"* (6:34), it is important to realize that he is not the only one God dealt with in such a way.

📖 Look up each of the passages listed below and identify the person who submitted to God's choice of "putting Him on like a garment."

Judges 3:9–10 _____

Judges 11:29 _____

Judges 13:24–25 _____

Judges 14:5–6 _____

Judges 14:19 _____

Judges 15:14 _____

It is interesting that this phrase is introduced with the first judge, Othniel, and is applied several times to Samson, the last judge of the book. In between we see it applied to Gideon and Jephthah. Although it isn't mentioned of every judge, it would certainly seem to be implied. It is also noteworthy that this is a repeated occurrence with Samson, indicating that it was a temporary experience.

This differs from the New Testament believer's relationship to the Spirit of God. In contrast with the Old Testament, the Spirit permanently indwells people today, and not just a select few, but all believers. There is this one similarity though: God still desires to call His people to His work and walk, and when they surrender to this call, they experience His empowering work in their lives.

📖 Read Judges 6:14–16 and 36. Does Gideon know that the Lord will deliver Israel through him?

_____

_____

What, then, is he really asking the Lord when he says *"If thou wilt deliver Israel through me. . ."*?

_____

_____

_____

Notice what Gideon says here: He asks, *"If Thou wilt deliver Israel through me,* **as Thou hast spoken. . ."** (emphasis added). What God had said was not in question. Gideon knew that God had said He would deliver Israel through him (Judges 6:14–16). Gideon's question is not, "God, what are you asking me to do?" but rather, "God, are you going to keep your end of the bargain?"

📖 Read Judges 6:36–40 and summarize Gideon's two requests.

_____

_____

In verse 39, how does Gideon approach God with his second request?

_____

_____

How did God respond each time?

_____

_____

How long would these "tests" have taken?

_____

Twice Gideon asks the Lord for a sign. First, he asks that the ground would be dry and the fleece wet, and the result is as he requested (so much so that a bowl full of dew is squeezed from the fleece). Second, he asks that the fleece would be dry and the ground wet with dew. Since each test revolved around the dew falling, we know that Gideon's request represented a two day delay. Again, our long-suffering Lord exhibited His patience with Gideon and his honest request for certainty.

GOD TEACHES GIDEON

Gideon

Today we will learn an important lesson about the people God uses. Even though God had already called Gideon and affirmed that calling in miraculous ways, that did not mean Gideon was ready for the task. God had to do a work *in* Gideon before He was ready to do a work *through* Gideon. God had some lessons for Gideon on how He delivers His people. Gideon, like us, was tempted to believe that God needs our help. Even though his army was small compared to the opponent, Gideon began with some level of trust in the army. In the end God was going to bring him to the place where there would be no one to trust but the Lord. Now we want to see what else we can learn from God's dealings with Gideon.

Read Judges 7:1–8. Why does the Lord say there are too many men with Gideon (v. 2)?

_____

_____

_____

_____

What solution does He provide in verse 3?

_____

_____

How many men were left?

_____

_____

God has to do a work in Gideon before He is ready to do a work through Gideon.

How did the Lord further reduce the possibility that Israel might think that they delivered themselves in their own power (vv. 4–6)?

_____

_____

_____

_____

What was the size of Gideon's army as a result of this test (6–8)?

_____

Did You Know?
GIDEON'S 300 MEN

Those who cupped the water in their hands could scan the area for enemies while they drank, as opposed to those who knelt down and put their faces to the water. The men selected were more alert than the average soldier.

As we saw in Judges 6:34–35, Gideon had assembled an army out of the tribes of Manasseh, Asher, Zebulun, and Naphtali. We learn here in verse 3 that this army numbered 32,000 at first. Verse 2 gives God's reason for downsizing: "_. . . lest Israel become boastful, saying 'My own power has delivered Me.'_" The Lord's first downsizing came when He had Gideon invite those who are afraid of the coming battle to leave. When the dust settled, two thirds of his army had disappeared. Though 22,000 soldiers departed, the army was still too large to suit the Lord. The second downsizing came when God instructed Gideon to send everyone home except those who lapped water from their hand like a dog. The quantity of Gideon's army was decimated. As a result, the army of 32,000 was reduced to 300—a downsizing of more than 99 percent. Finally, God had an army that was useable for His purpose.

📖 Read Judges 7:9–11. What two instructions did God give Gideon (vv. 9–10)?

_____

_____

_____

What assurances did He give Gideon (vv. 9b, 11a)?

_____

_____

_____

Even with the assurances coming directly from God's mouth, what did Gideon do (v. 11b)?

_____

_____

God told Gideon to **1)** go down against the camp, and **2)** take your servant if you are afraid. God assured Gideon by telling him that He had given the camp into his hands and that he would be strengthened by what he heard the enemy say. Once again we see that God is willing to help us trust Him in our weaknesses. Out of fear, Gideon took his servant with him to the camp. Out of obedience, he secretly entered the camp of the Midianites and heard what the enemy was saying.

📖 Read Judges 7:12. Humanly speaking, what were the odds of Gideon winning this battle with his three hundred men?

_____

God brought Gideon to a point of total desperation and dependence upon Him. There was no way in the world, without God, that Gideon or his three hundred men would come out alive. In this camp, preparing for the impending battle, were ruthless, heartless warriors too great in number to even count.

APPLY Relate a time in your life when God had you in a position where the only way to have victory was if He did something miraculous.

_____

_____

_____

_____

📖 Read Judges 7:13–14. Summarize what Gideon heard in the camp.

_____

_____

_____

_____

What was his reaction (v. 15)?

_____

_____

_____

In this text, God is patiently reassuring Gideon once again. He allows Gideon to overhear one man relating a dream to another, and the interpretation of that dream confirmed through the mouth of a Midianite that God had given the camp into Gideon's hand. God sovereignly used an enemy to reveal His ways. How patient and understanding the Lord is! When Gideon heard this _"he bowed in worship"_ and then declared to the camp of Israel, _"the LORD has given the camp of Midian into your hands."_

📖 Read Judges 7:16–20. What did each man take into battle (v. 16)?

_____

_____

_____

What method would they use for their attack (vv. 17–18)?

_____

_____

_____

What weapons did they take into battle?

_____

Put Yourself In Their Shoes
GIDEON'S FIRST RESPONSE

When God allowed Gideon to overhear the discussion of the Midianites, He was reassuring Gideon's weak faith. Gideon's first response was to bow _"in worship."_ What is your first response when you are blessed by the Lord—is it worship or do you take His blessings for granted?

God's plan, which Gideon relates to the three hundred men in his army, is for them to surround the camp, in unison break the pitchers which hid the light of their lamps, blow their trumpets and shout, *"A sword for the LORD and for Gideon!"* There is no mention of them carrying swords or weapons of any kind. In fact, since they held the torch with one hand and the trumpet with the other, they wouldn't have had a hand free to use a sword if they had carried them.

📖 Read Judges 7:21–25. What was the result of the attack?

_____

_____

God used the noise to strike fear and confusion into the enemy so that they fought against one another in their attempt to flee. Gideon called men from the tribes to pursue the fleeing army, and the whole of the Midianites were routed that day to the glory of God.

With everything that was against him, Gideon carried the one weapon that would assure victory: the Lord. Everything God commanded Gideon concerning the battle was completely unreasonable as far as human logic is concerned. Most of us would have been tempted to respond, "But Lord! This is war! Don't be ridiculous!" But Gideon trusted God and saw great victory because of it. God has given us brains to reason with, and He expects us to use them. But we lose much if we trade our own understanding for God's "unreasonable" directions.

Gideon's story is a simple one—God used a small, insignificant man to bring about a mighty victory. God chose Gideon for the same reason He wanted a smaller army: He wanted everyone to know that it was not the army who conquered, nor the man who led them, but God who brought deliverance to Israel.

> **With everything that was against him, Gideon carried the one weapon that would assure victory: the Lord.**

Gideon **DAY FIVE**

FOR ME TO FOLLOW GOD

God worked in mighty ways in and through Gideon's life, changing him into a man of faith and changing the world around Gideon through him. But God was not just interested in Gideon. He wants to work in the lives of each of His children. How can we open up our lives to be useful to Him as well?

📖 Read Judges 6:11, 15, 27, 36–37 and 7:9–11. What characterized Gideon? Check all characteristics that apply in the list below.

___fear	___self-doubt
___courage	___inadequacy
___determination	___audacity
___daring	___cowardice
___need for reassurance	___confidence

APPLY Describe a time when you've felt inadequate for a task set before you.

_____

_____

_____

_____

How do you tend to respond in these situations?

_____

_____

_____

📖 Read Judges 6:16, 34, 38, 40, and 7:2–7, 9–15. What characterized God's response to Gideon's fears and doubts?

_____

_____

_____

📖 Read Hebrews 11:32–34. What was the result when God's strength was added to Gideon's weakness, and how did Gideon tap into God's strength?

_____

_____

_____

_____

What does Hebrews 11:6 tell us about faith?

_____

_____

_____

Faith is simply believing God is Who He says He is, and believing He will do what He says He will do. It's taking God at His word. Our only true success and victory in life is in pleasing God, and faith is the one way we can do that.

The world has all the wrong answers. Confidence in ourselves is not the answer—all our confidence should be in Him. Self-assurance is not the answer, for He is our assurance. And our attempts to control our own lives isn't the answer: rather than trying to control situations or our reaction to them, we should yield everything in our lives to His control. The world would have us settle for what _we_ can accomplish. But why should we, when there is so much more God wants to accomplish in and through us? His ways are so much greater.

> "...without faith it is impossible to please Him, for he who comes to God must believe that He is, and that He is a rewarder of those who seek Him."
>
> **Hebrews 11:6**

📖 Read 2 Corinthians 12:9 and James 1:5. How does God say He will respond to us in our inadequacy?

_____

_____

_____

📖 According to Ephesians 3:16, 20 and Philippians 4:13, what will the results be in our lives?

_____

_____

_____

Our only true success and victory in life is in pleasing God.

God fully knows our inadequacy, and He wants us to realize that without Him, we are completely inadequate. He, however, is completely adequate, and His strength is glorified in our weakness. All too often, we just let our own "strength" get in the way.

APPLY Are you choosing to depend on God instead of your own human strengths so that God can reveal His strength in your weakness?

_____

_____

_____

_____

_____

_____

"The things impossible with men are possible with God." Luke 18:27

The work of the Christian life is not to achieve something for God. The work of the Christian life is to let God have us and His way with our lives. He will accomplish what He wants through us if we yield to Him.

There is a song aptly titled, "Little is much when God is in it." God doesn't want us to overestimate ourselves, but neither does He want us to underestimate what He can do in and through our lives. In Luke 18:27, Christ said: _"The things impossible with men are possible with God."_ We can accomplish nothing of true value in and of ourselves, but God is in the business of doing great, humanly impossible things. With Him, all things are possible!

Spend some time in prayer with the Lord right now.

 Lord, how can I be filled with Your power and strength unless I am emptied of my own? I want to be small, that I may be usable by You. Search every hidden corner of my heart and sweep out any accomplishments of my own abilities that I may be clinging to. I would find all my sufficiency and confidence in You. I thank You that You are patient with my foolishness. Forgive my doubts and honor the true seeking of my heart. I choose to follow You by faith with my whole life. Teach me how. In Jesus' name, Amen.

Write out your own prayer to the Lord, and seek His strength.

_____

_____

_____

_____

_____

_____

_____

_____

_____

God is in the business of doing humanly impossible things.

Notes

THE DOWNWARD SPIRAL
OF SIN

Samson appears on the scene at a dark point in Israel's history, after the nation had settled in the Promised Land, but before the time of the kings. The dismal refrain of the book of Judges is reflected in the repeated statement, *"In those days there was no king in Israel; every man did what was right in his own eyes"* (Judges 17:6; 18:1; 19:1; 21:25). Because there was no king and no authority, Israel would stray from God, forgetting the law. Then God would bring another nation against them as a means of getting their attention. After that, God would raise up a judge to point them back to the Lord. Samson was one of these judges. He was set apart for this task from his mother's womb. We want to look at how Samson succeeded and prospered when he followed God, and how much it cost him when he failed to follow Him.

> **"... every man did what was right in his own eyes."**
> **Judges 17:6**

WHERE DOES HE FIT?

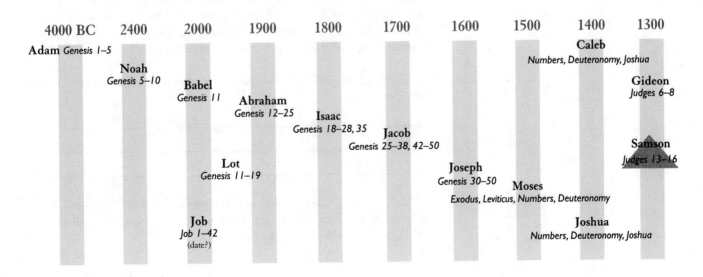

SIN TAKES YOU FURTHER THAN YOU THOUGHT YOU'D STRAY

Although many judges had delivered Israel from their oppressors, again and again they would stray. When Samson came on the scene, Israel had been dominated by the Philistines for forty years as a consequence of their sin (Judges 13:1). We will begin by looking at Samson's God-given life purpose, and how he strayed from it.

📖 Read Judges 13:1–24. According to verse 5, what was to be Samson's purpose in life?

_____

_____

What restrictions were placed on Samson and his mother (vv. 4–5)?

_____

_____

Samson was a child of blessing to a barren woman. The life purpose laid out for Samson was to *"begin to deliver Israel from the hands of the Philistines."* His mother was told *"not to drink wine or strong drink, nor eat any unclean thing"* during the pregnancy. The implication is that this would defile Samson. Samson was called to be a *"Nazirite"* from the womb which, in addition to the restriction of no razor touching his head, would include drinking no alcohol and not touching a dead person (Numbers 6).

In chapter 14, after he reached adulthood, we begin to see Samson's weaknesses coming to the surface.

📖 Read Judges 14:1–4. What is Samson's criteria for selecting a wife?

_____

_____

In Judges 14:3 we see that Samson's main criteria for selecting this woman was that, as he puts it, *"She looks good to me."* To him, her character was not important (she was from the pagan Philistines), nor was the fact that she was not an Israelite. All that mattered to him was how she looked.

Even though Samson's motives were impure, what does verse 4 tell us about God's intentions?

_____

_____

_____

God had a sovereign purpose in mind and worked through Samson's desires so He could use him against the Philistines, though, as we will see, He would not allow those desires to prosper.

Did You Know?
THE NAZIRITE VOW

The word *"Nazirite"* means "separated," and referred specifically to "one who was separated unto the Lord." By the terms of the vow, a man or woman could voluntarily separate himself unto the Lord for a specific period of time, even for life. He did not, however, become a hermit, separating himself from society. Samson and Samuel (1 Samuel 1:11, 28) are two notable Nazirites. It is also thought that John the Baptist may have been a Nazirite (see Luke 1:15), and that perhaps this was the nature of the vow associated with Paul (see Acts 21:23–26).

📖 Read Judges 14:10–20. What was the end result of Samson's wedding feast (v. 20)?

_____

_____

_____

Samson had a calling, but he also had a weakness—women. In the narrative of his failed attempt to marry we see that most likely he violated two of the three restrictions the Nazirite vow demanded of his life. In preparation for his marriage, 14:10 says Samson *"made a feast"* at his father-in-law's house as *"the young men customarily did this."* The Philistine custom for making a feast included getting drunk (Violation #1: drinking alcohol).

At this feast Samson made a bet that no one could guess a riddle about his experience on the way there. Because his wife-to-be tricked the information out of him, he lost the bet and owed thirty changes of clothes. In his anger he went out and killed thirty men of Ashkelon and then took their clothes to pay his debt (Violation #2: touching a dead person). Probably because of Samson's anger, his wife was given to someone else.

Samson's anger over losing his fiancée may have driven him to revenge, but God used Samson not only to kill these thirty men, but also moved him to use foxes to set their crops on fire (Judges 15). In the war that followed a thousand more Philistines died. The last verse of chapter 15 tells us that for the next twenty years Samson judged Israel. Apparently the Philistines left Israel alone as long as they stayed in their own region.

In chapter 16 we see that though Samson was twenty years older, he was no better at denying his flesh.

📖 Read Judges 16:1–3. What did Samson do (v. 1)?

_____

_____

How did the Philistines respond?

_____

_____

_____

Samson went into Gaza and found a harlot for his fleshly purpose. Gaza was in the region of the Philistines. Samson had violated the neutral zone to satisfy his lust. When our desire is to follow our flesh, we look for opportunities. In following his lusts instead of following God, Samson not only crossed the boundaries of the Philistines, he crossed the boundary of God and moved into immorality. The Philistines took advantage of this opportunity to try and kill their old enemy. Though this move into Gaza put Samson in danger, he seemed to escape with no consequences. But looking closely we see that this stepping across the line kindled his lusts, and he went lower than simply trying to marry an unbeliever.

Samson's weakness took him further than he intended to stray, and there were consequences. It is important to notice that for twenty years it appeared Samson's weakness for women lay dormant. But when he chose to cross the line (and sin is *always* a choice) his lusts were awakened. Samson didn't seem to realize that though the Philistines did not catch him, his own flesh would.

God had a specific purpose and calling for Samson's life (to deliver Israel from the Philistines), but Samson chose to follow his own desires into the land of the Philistines.

APPLY Describe an incident in your life when you strayed from what you knew God wanted you to do by choosing to pursue what you wanted instead.

_____

_____

_____

_____

_____

_____

Samson faced the consequences of his straying, but we also see God's overruling hand working to accomplish His purposes in relation to Israel and the Philistines.

How has God worked to accomplish *His* purposes in your life—maybe even in spite of yourself?

_____

_____

_____

_____

It is important to realize that though God wants to use us, He will accomplish His will—with or without us. Sometimes He will use us even if we are unwilling, but in our unwillingness, we miss the blessings He wants to give us and the intimate daily relationship He desires to have with us.

Sin Keeps You Longer Than You Thought You'd Stay

Samson DAY TWO

We have seen that Samson had a divine call on his life, but that he also had a very human weakness for women. Sin had taken him farther than he had ever intended to stray—he went from attempting to marry an unbeliever because she "looked good," to an immoral relationship with a Philistine harlot. Now we will see that saying "yes" to his flesh would keep him longer than he had ever intended to stay. It seems obvious from the story that follows that Samson simply would not control his lust.

Sin is always a choice.

📖 Read Judges 16:4–9, and list everything you learn about Delilah and her character.

_____

_____

_____

_____

_____

_____

The text tells us that Samson _"loved"_ Delilah. The Hebrew word _'ahar_ can refer to the love between family members or friends, to longing and desire, and to physical attraction (see Genesis 29:18; 2 Samuel 13:1; Esther 2:17). In and of itself the word used here for love does not describe immoral actions, but the context of Judges 16 confirms the reality of an improper relationship, especially since Samson and Delilah were apparently not married. The text doesn't tell us if Delilah is a Philistine, but we do know that the area in which she lived was under Philistine control, and her receptivity to their plot shows where her sympathies lay. We see her low character revealed not only in the immorality of their relationship, but in her greed for ill-gotten gain and her willingness to sell out Samson.

📖 Read Judges 16:4–14. Summarize the first three requests Delilah made of Samson.

_____

_____

How did Samson avoid each of the three traps?

1. _____

_____

2. _____

_____

3. _____

_____

Three times Delilah asked Samson the secret of his strength, but Samson eluded her traps. The **first** time Samson lied and said if he were bound with fresh cords (bowstring made from twisted gut), he would lose his strength. The **second** lie was for him to be bound with new, unused ropes. Lie **number three** was for his hair to be woven into the loom.

🛑 **APPLY** Considering how many times Delilah attempted to trap Samson, why do you think Samson let this relationship go on after Delilah had proved that she couldn't be trusted?

_____

_____

_____

_____

Did You Know?

ELEVEN HUNDRED PIECES OF SILVER

The bribe to Delilah was eleven hundred pieces (shekels) of silver from each of the five lords of the Philistines. This would be a total of about 170 pounds of silver. If Delilah was disloyal to God by having an immoral relationship with Samson, it is no surprise that she was disloyal to Samson with such an offer of money.

We have to wonder why Samson stayed when Delilah's unfaithfulness to him was obvious. Surely Samson was not so naive as to overlook the fact that each time he told her a made-up secret, she tried to use it against him. There are two probable reasons he did not leave her: either he was so confident he could escape any trap she set, that he stayed to enjoy her pleasures (she was hired to *"entice"* him—16:5), or he was so dulled by sin that he lost all discernment.

📖 Now read Judges 16:15–17. What did Delilah do differently this time (v. 15)?

_____

_____

_____

Why do you think Samson responded so foolishly, by revealing the true secret of his strength?

_____

_____

_____

Up until now Samson had eluded Delilah's traps through his deception, but the text tells us that Delilah changed her question to *"How can you say, 'I love you,' when your heart is not with me? You have deceived me these three times and have not told me where your great strength is."* She appealed to the emotional attachment he had developed. To this point Samson had been playing with sin, convinced that he could handle it. But **he had stayed in the relationship too long**, and in a moment of weakness his flesh got the best of him and he foolishly revealed his secret.

Sin had taken Samson further than he had ever intended to stray. First, He left the safety of his countrymen for the pleasures of women in the Philistine territory. Second, he wanted to marry an unbelieving Philistine woman only because she looked good. Then he stepped lower and had an immoral interlude with a Philistine prostitute. He should have left Philistine women alone after that, but he escaped the immediate consequences and deceived himself into thinking that he had gotten away with his sin.

With Delilah he had stepped lower still. He developed an illicit emotional attachment to her. He should have left after the first betrayal, but he escaped her trap and thought he could handle it. Pleasure dulled his perceptions. It should have been obvious after the second trap that she could not be trusted, but Samson thought he had things under control. He surely knew he was doing wrong, but he thought he was managing the problem.

The third trap still did not bring him to his senses. And then she began to wear him down with her appeals. Scripture admonishes, *"Flee immorality!"* (1 Corinthians 6:18). At every step Samson should have fled, but instead he stayed too long.

Playing with sin in your life, whether it's as egregious as Samson's or it seems relatively innocent, is like staying on the sand bar when the tide is coming in. You know the tide always comes in, and you think you'll know before its too late. But it creeps up on you, and before you know it, you're trapped.

Samson thought he had things under control; he thought he was managing the problem.

This is true in our lives as well. Sin not only takes us further than we thought we would stray, it also keeps us longer than we thought we would stay.

What could Samson have done to avoid staying too long?

_____

_____

The way to avoid getting bogged down in sin is to turn to God in the very moment that you face the temptation. *"No temptation has overtaken you but such as is common to man; and God is faithful, Who will not allow you to be tempted beyond what you are able, but with the temptation will provide the way of escape also, that you may be able to endure it"* (1 Corinthians 10:13). Being faced with temptation is not a sin, but nurturing the temptation is (James 1:14–15).

There is only one way to stop the downward spiral of sin, and that is to repent. Through the power of Christ within you, seek God and obedience to His ways with your whole heart.

SIN COSTS YOU MORE THAN YOU THOUGHT YOU'D PAY

There were terrible consequences for Samson's lack of repentance. As we look at them we will see how much his sin would end up costing him—so much more than he ever thought he would pay.

📖 Read Judges 16:18–22, 25. List at least five things that Samson's sin has cost him.

_____

_____

_____

_____

_____

God exposed Samson's sin, and he was caught. **First,** he lost his supernatural strength (v. 19). **Second,** he lost his discernment—sin had so stained him that he did not even realize that the blessing of God was no longer on his life (v. 20). **Third,** he lost his eyesight as they gouged his eyes out (v. 21a). **Fourth,** he lost his freedom—he was taken captive, and his life was reduced to the job of a mule (v. 21b). **Fifth,** he lost his testimony—His sin and fall enabled the Philistines to believe their god had delivered him into their hands (vv. 22–24). **Last** but not least, he lost his dignity. His captors used him for entertainment and amusement (v. 25).

"...God is faithful, Who will not allow you to be tempted beyond what you are able, but with the temptation will provide the way of escape also, that you may be able to endure it."
1 Corinthians 10:13

Samson DAY THREE

📖 Why do you think cutting Samson's hair took away his strength? Compare the story you just read in Judges with Numbers 6:1–8.

_____

_____

_____

_____

_____

Samson's strength was in God, not his hair, but his long hair was a sign of his Nazirite vow to God. It was the only one of the three components of the vow he had not yet violated. He apparently violated the command forbidding him from drinking wine when he drank at his wedding party with the Philistines (Judges 14:10). This restriction even prohibited him from eating grapes. It is significant that the home of Delilah (Sorek) is named after a particular kind of vine that produced purple grapes for which it became famous. He violated the prohibition against touching something dead when he ate from the lion's carcass (14:5–9) and again when he removed the clothing from the thirty Philistines (14:19). Samson's strength left him not just because his hair had been cut, but because in allowing his hair to be cut, he had completely violated his vows as a Nazirite.

Samson had a choice between God and things of eternal significance, and his flesh and the gratification of the moment. Whenever we choose to follow our fleshly desires instead of following God there is always a price to be paid.

🛑 **APPLY** Why do you think that there are personal consequences when we sin?

_____

_____

_____

_____

_____

God is not an old man standing over us with a big stick waiting for us to get "out of line." He is a loving Father who wants us to grow up to be who He created us to be—conformed to the image of His Son (Romans 8:28–29). He wants us to make the right choice because all of our choices affect other people, our walk with Him, and the attributes of Christ that He is trying to work out in our lives. If all God cared about was **what we did**, He would have made us puppets on a string. He also cares about **who we are,** and the things we do reflect who we are. He gave us His Word to show us who He intends for us to be, to give us freedom to choose and consequences to help us make the right choice.

Samson eventually paid a high price for his choices. When we look at our world, we realize that we all pay a price for the choices we make.

If all God cared about was what we do, He would have made us puppets on a string. He also cares about who we are.

APPLY What would you say to someone faced with the same kinds of choices that Samson faced?

_____

_____

_____

_____

_____

_____

Do you apply these same principles to yourself when you're faced with a choice between God and your fleshly desires? (Choose which one best applies to you.)

_____ a) I'm learning how to apply these principles more every day.

_____ b) Almost never

_____ c) When it's convenient

_____ d) When others are watching

_____ e) When I've been consistently studying the Bible and praying

_____ f) Yes

It may look like we get away with sin for a time, but the consequences will show up eventually in one way or another. The consequences Samson faced can all be traced to what is perhaps the saddest statement of the entire story: _"But he did not know that the Lord had departed from him."_ Samson was not even following God closely enough to notice His departure. And without God, Samson was without everything truly good in his life. Everything truly good in our lives comes from God, and when we forsake Him and His ways for momentary pleasure, we also forsake His blessings.

📖 Read Judges 16:22. What happened?

_____

_____

_____

What significance do you see in the growth of Samson's hair?

_____

_____

_____

As mentioned earlier, Samson's strength was never in his hair. His hair growing out did not automatically bring his strength back, but it may have served to remind him that not all of the damage done had to be permanent. Notice, his strength did not return when his hair grew back, but when he called to the Lord (vv. 28–30).

Samson's sin was overt. His weakness was lust. Perhaps your weakness is in a different area; but if you do not let God control it, your sin will control

> **"But he did not know that the Lord had departed from him."**
>
> **Judges 16:20**

you. Samson's sin **took him further** than he intended to stray, it **kept him longer** than he intended to stay, and it **cost him more** than he intended to pay. If our story ended here it would be dismal indeed.

GOD'S ABUNDANT MERCIES ARE FRESH EVERY DAY

Though sin cost Samson so much, the good news from his life is that we never sink so low that we can no longer repent. There is a downward spiral to sin, and the longer we play with it, the more it will cost us, but thank God, his abundant mercies are fresh every day!

☐ Looking back at Judges 13—16, briefly summarize all the ways Samson had violated God's will and law.

_____

_____

_____

_____

_____

_____

When we view Samson's life and look for the wrong turns he made, we see that **first,** he sought a wife among the uncircumcised in violation of the law. **Second,** he committed immorality—something expressly forbidden. **Third,** he broke his Nazirite vows, something (in his case) designed to be lifelong. **Fourth,** even though he had to know his actions were wrong and dangerous, he refused to repent of his immoral relationship with Delilah. **Finally,** he failed Israel, whom he was called to lead, and set an example before them not of obedience to God, but of disobedience.

Samson had utterly fallen from God's purposes for him, but was God through with Him? Does God ever wash His hands of us?

☐ Read Ephesians 2:1–5. What does this tell you about God's character and His dealings with us?

_____

_____

_____

_____

"BUT GOD. . . ." These two words alone show the character of our loving Father. He is and always has been a God of *"mercy."* God regards our present condition, and His mercy is concerned with alleviating the consequences of sin. Mercy prompts God's grace, so how was God's mercy going to be seen in Samson's life?

"But God, being rich in mercy, because of His great love with which He loved us, even when we were dead in our transgressions, made us alive together with Christ (by grace you have been saved). . . ."
Ephesians 2:4–5

📖 Read Judges 16:23–27 and briefly describe the setting unto which Samson is brought.

_____

_____

_____

_____

_____

During a worship celebration to the pagan god, Dagon, Samson was called to entertain the people present. The Hebrew word used literally means he was their laughter and indicates they "made sport" with him, or mocked and ridiculed him. He appeared before a packed house of, and was providentially placed beside the pillars of the building.

📖 Look at Judges 16:28–29. What did Samson do?

_____

_____

_____

_____

The most important thing in the final incident in Samson's life is that Samson "_called to the LORD._" If we are of God's family, we never sink so low that we cannot call to Him.

In verse 30, what was the result?

_____

_____

_____

Who did Samson kill (vv. 27, 30)?

_____

_____

Did he fulfill God's purpose for his life (review Judges 13:5)?

_____

_____

God heard Samson's prayers and answered them, giving him back his strength. When he pushed down the pillars of the building, the destruction was total. Even though he died in the disaster, in his death Samson killed more Philistines than he did in his life, and among the dead in the building were "_all the lords of the Philistines._" God was still able to use him as a deliverer and judge when he repented and called to the Lord.

Why do you think Samson finally called out to God?

_____

_____

_____

Sometimes we have to lose what we think is ours in order to recognize that we've always needed a Savior.

God allowed Samson to scrape bottom and lose everything he had—his position as a judge, his strength, his sight, his family, his freedom, and his dignity. Samson must have finally realized that the only resource he ever really had was God. Sometimes we have to lose what we think is ours in order to recognize that we've always needed a Savior.

APPLY Has there been a point in your life when God allowed you to lose something in order to realize your need for Him. If so, describe that below.

_____

_____

_____

_____

_____

📖 Look up the following verses and list God's response when we call on His Name.

Psalm 4:1

_____

Psalm 18:3

_____

Psalm 50:15

_____

Psalm 91:15

_____

Jeremiah 29:12–13

_____

Jeremiah 33:3

_____

Joel 2:32

_____

Romans 10:13

_____

It is never too late to return to the Lord!

Calling on God does not necessarily relieve you from the circumstances in which your sin has put you. It also does not mean that all relationships will automatically be restored. But it does mean that you've tapped into the one relationship that is the true source of every good thing. Call on the Lord, but don't wait, like Samson, until the last minute. Don't wait for physical desperation. We should follow God so closely that we become spiritually desperate when there is any distance at all between us and Him.

Like the nation he was supposed to lead, Samson had to learn the hard way that it is never worthwhile to rebel against God. Samson's story doesn't necessarily have a happy ending, but it does end in hope instead of despair. And the good news from his life, and his death, is that even when we fail, God's abundant mercies are fresh every day.

FOR ME TO FOLLOW GOD

As we look at the life of Samson, we see certain principles that are timeless. They are as relevant today as they were in Samson's day. As we seek to make these principles personal, it is essential that we take time to look to God to apply them to our lives.

Sin took Samson farther than he ever thought he would stray.

Sin never tells you the whole story. It starts with one relatively innocent sounding choice. "What's the big deal?" "It won't hurt just this once." "Nobody will know." "You need to try it at least once!" How many alcoholics (liars, drug addicts, fornicators, etc.) have heard these statements and wish they had made the right choice the first time?

APPLY   Describe an occasion in your life when a "small" sin took you further than you'd intended.

_____

_____

_____

_____

_____

Sin kept him longer than he ever thought he'd stay.

When we make the wrong choice, we immediately carry a burden that God never intended for us to bear. The next time the temptation is before us, it's harder to make the right choice. Each time it becomes easier and easier to make the wrong choice. This is the downward spiral of sin!

Sin cost him more than he ever thought he'd pay.

📖 Read Romans 6:16–23. When we sin, what do we become (v. 16)?

_____

_____

The trap was set, and you got caught! Now what you originally saw as "freedom to do as you wanted" has actually made you a prisoner—a slave to your own sinful desires.

What is the result when people become *"slaves to impurity and to lawlessness"* (v. 19)?

_____

_____

What you originally saw as "freedom to do as you wanted" has actually made you a prisoner— a slave to your own sinful desires.

What is the outcome of sin (vv. 16, 21, 23)?

_____

_____

Victory is not you overcoming sin; victory is Jesus overcoming you!

The price tag can come in many forms: an adulterer losing his family, the liar losing the respect of others, or an alcoholic trading his family, home and job for one more drink. Does every first drink end with a homeless person? Of course not. The price tag may not be that obvious. The price tag for alcohol consumption may show up in different ways: hangovers in the morning, DUI tickets, or spending a few nights in jail on occasion. But the outcome of alcohol abuse as well as with any other sin is always death: the death of hopes and dreams, the death of peace, the death of relationships, and eventually physical death. So, is there any hope? How do you get out? Where is the escape hatch?

Victory is not you overcoming sin, victory is Jesus overcoming you!

📖 Read Romans 6:22. What is the alternative to being a slave to sin?

_____

_____

A person can learn to change their behavior through various programs, but the only way to know true freedom (being free from the power of sin) is to know the One who is willing and able to free you from your slavery. You have a choice to handcuff yourself to sin, or to handcuff yourself to Christ. There is hope and it is found in Christ.

Most of us know how we handle sin. We're trying to make the right choices, but eventually we blow it, and the guilt hits us. We feel horrible, so we vow to God—"I'm sorry God. I will never do that again!" And we try harder. But sooner or later, we blow it again, and the cycle continues. "God, I will never, ever do that again!" And we try even harder.

Surrender is giving the Holy Spirit complete access to your life.

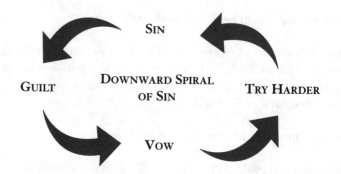

But there is a way to break that cycle: it's called surrender. Surrender is giving the Holy Spirit complete access to your life. When faced with temptation, if we immediately surrender to God rather than the temptation, His power will carry us safely through.

📖 Read 1 Corinthians 10:13. What will God not allow?

_____

_____

What will He provide?

_____

And why will He do these things?

_____

_____

What does "_faithful_" mean?

_____

_____

God can be trusted 100 percent to do these things for us! If you respond to temptation with the right choice, you don't have to pay the high cost of sin—the consequences. This is God's design. It's all about depending on Him, not to take all temptation out of your life, but to give you His power to correctly respond to it. We can't consistently resist temptation in our own strength, only His strength in us can do that. And He is completely dependable.

When we do sin, we need to deal with it the right way. Dealing with sin is as basic to our spiritual lives as breathing is to our physical lives. We exhale confession—agreeing with God about our sin, and repentance—turning to God and away from our sin (Proverbs 28:13). And we inhale the Holy Spirit's control of our lives.

📖 Read 1 John 5:14–15. What do we know about God?

_____

_____

_____

What does Ephesians 5:18 command us to do?

_____

_____

APPLY What do these two scriptures tell you about your ability to be filled (controlled) by the Holy Spirit?

_____

_____

When we become Christians, the Holy Spirit comes to live in our lives **permanently.** His control of every area of our lives is what empowers us to resist any temptation that confronts us. But when we choose to take control in any area, we face the temptation in our own strength alone. It is God's will that we be continually filled with the Spirit and His power. When we choose to once again surrender control of our lives to God, His power neutralizes the power of sin in our lives.

Dealing with sin is as basic to our spiritual lives as breathing is to our physical lives.

As we are becoming conformed to the image of Christ, we break the downward spiral of sin in our lives.

Within the context of spiritual warfare in our own lives, what does 2 Corinthians 10:3–5 tell us to do with our thoughts?

_____

_____

What does Colossians 3:1–2 tell us to do?

_____

_____

_____

"Take every thought captive to the obedience of Christ." *"Set your mind on things above. . . ."* Paul obviously thought it was important for us to saturate our minds with the things of God—His Word. And as we are becoming conformed to the image of Christ (having His mind), we break the downward spiral of sin in our lives.

Remember, God's abundant mercies are fresh every day!

Spend some time in prayer with the Lord right now.

Lord, forgive my casual attitude towards the sin in my life. I want to follow You so closely that the slightest distraction which draws my eye from You is painful to my soul. Make me sensitive to sin, to anything which distracts my heart from You. Thank You for Your amazing, inexhaustible grace in my life. I do not want to take it lightly. I choose to surrender control of every area of my life to You. Hold me to that choice, Lord, when the things of this world seem good to me. Help me to recognize that only You can truly satisfy my heart. In Jesus' name, Amen.

Write out your prayer to the Lord of mercies.

_____

_____

_____

_____

_____

_____

_____

_____

_____

_____

_____

Notes

Notes

How to Follow God

Starting the Journey

DID YOU KNOW that you have been on God's heart and mind for a long, long time? Even before time existed you were on His mind. He has always wanted you to know Him in a personal, purposeful relationship. He has a purpose for your life and it is founded upon His great love for you. You can be assured it is a good purpose and it lasts forever. Our time on this earth is only the beginning. God has a grand design that goes back into eternity past and reaches into eternity future. What is that design?

The Scriptures are clear about God's design for man—God created man to live and walk in oneness with Himself. Oneness with God means being in a relationship that is totally unselfish, totally satisfying, totally secure, righteous and pure in every way. That's what we were created for. If we walked in that kind of relationship with God we would glorify Him and bring pleasure to Him. Life would be right! Man was meant to live that way—pleasing to God and glorifying Him (giving a true estimate of who God is). Adam sinned and shattered his oneness with God. Ever since, man has come short of the glory of God: man does not and cannot please God or give a true estimate of God. Life is not right until a person is right with God. That is very clear as we look at the many people who walked across the pages of Scripture, both Old and New Testaments.

JESUS CHRIST came as the solution for this dilemma. Jesus Christ **is** the glory of God—the true estimate of who God is in every way. He pleased His Father in everything He did and said, and He came to restore oneness with God. He came to give man His power and grace to walk in oneness with God, to follow Him day by day enjoying the relationship for which he was created. In the process, man could begin to present a true picture of Who God is and experience knowing Him personally. You may be asking, "How do these facts impact my life today? How does this become real to me now? How can I begin the journey of following God in this way?" To come to know God personally means you must choose to receive Jesus Christ as your personal Savior and Lord.

- First of all, you must **admit** that you have sinned, that you are not walking in oneness with God, not pleasing Him or glorifying Him in your life (Romans 3:23; 6:23; 8:5-8).

- It means **repenting** of that sin—changing your mind, **turning to** God and **turning away from** sin—and by faith **receiving** His forgiveness based on His death on the Cross for you (Romans 3:21-26; 1 Peter 3:18).

- It means opening your life to **receive Him** as your living, resurrected Lord and Savior (John 1:12). He has promised to come and indwell you by His Spirit and live in you as the Savior and Master of your life (John 14:16-21; Romans 14:7-9).

- He wants to **live His life through you**—conforming you to His image, bearing His fruit through you and giving you power to reign in life (John 15:1,4-8; Romans 5:17; 7:4; 8:29, 37).

You can come to Him now. In your own words, simply tell Him you want to know Him personally and you willingly repent of your sin and receive His forgiveness and His life. Tell Him you want to follow Him forever (Romans 10:9-10, 13). *Welcome to the Family of God and to the greatest journey of all!!!*

WALKING ON THE JOURNEY

HOW DO WE FOLLOW HIM DAY BY DAY? Remember, Christ has given those who believe in Him *everything* pertaining to life and godliness, so that we no longer have to be slaves to our "flesh" and its corruption (2 Peter 1:3-4). Day by day He wants to empower us to live a life of love and joy, pleasing to Him and rewarding to us. That's why Ephesians 5:18 tells us to *"be filled with the Spirit"*—keep on being controlled by the Spirit who lives in you. He knows exactly what we need each day and we can trust Him to lead us (Proverbs 3:5-6). So how can we cooperate with Him in this journey together?

To walk with Him *day by day* means ...

- reading and listening to His Word day by day (Luke 10:39, 42; Colossians 3:16; Psalm 19:7-14; 119:9).

- spending time talking to Him in prayer (Philippians 4:6-7).

- realizing that God is God and you are not, and the role that means He has in your life.

This allows Him to work through your life as you fellowship, worship, pray and learn with other believers (Acts 2:42), and serve in the good works He has prepared for us to do—telling others who Jesus is and what His Word says, teaching and encouraging others, giving to help meet needs, helping others, etc. (Ephesians 2:10).

God's goal for each of us is that we be conformed to the image of His Son, Jesus Christ (Romans 8:29). But none of us will reach that goal of perfection until we are with Him in Heaven, for then *"we shall be like Him, because we shall see Him just as He is"* (1 John 3:2). For now, He wants us to follow Him faithfully, learning more each day. Every turn in the road, every trial and every blessing, is designed to bring us to a new depth of surrender to the Lord and His ways. He not only wants us to do His will, He desires that we surrender to His will *His way*. That takes trust—trust in His character, His plan and His goals (Proverbs 3:5-6).

As you continue this journey, and perhaps you've been following Him for a while, you must continue to listen carefully and follow closely. We never graduate from that. That sensitivity to God takes moment by moment surrender, dying to the impulses of our flesh to go our own way, saying no to the temptations of Satan to doubt God and His Word, and refusing the lures of the world to be unfaithful to the Lord who gave His life for us.

God desires that each of us come to maturity as sons and daughters: to that point where we are fully satisfied in Him and His ways, fully secure in His sovereign love, and walking in the full measure of His purity and holiness. If we are to clearly present the image of Christ for all to see, it will take daily surrender and daily seeking to follow Him wherever He leads, however He gets there (Luke 9:23-25). It's a faithful walk of trust through time into eternity. And it is worth everything. Trust Him. Listen carefully. *Follow closely*.

Other Books in the *Following God*™ Bible Character Study Series

Life Principles from the Kings of the Old Testament

Characters include Saul, David, Solomon, Jereboam I, Asa, Ahab, Jehoshaphat, Hezekiah, Josiah, Zerubbabel & Ezra, Nehemiah, and "The True King in Israel."
ISBN 0-89957-301-0   256 pages

Life Principles from the Prophets of the Old Testament

Characters include Samuel, Elijah, Elisha, Jonah, Hosea, Isaiah, Micah, Jeremiah, Habakkuk, Daniel, Haggai, and "Christ the Prophet."
ISBN 0-89957-303-7   224 pages

Life Principles from the New Testament Men of Faith

Characters include John the Baptist, Peter, John, Thomas, James, Barnabas, Paul, Paul's Companions, Timothy, and "The Son of Man."
ISBN 0-89957-304-5   208 pages

Life Principles from the Women of the Bible (Book One)

Characters include Eve, Sarah, Miriam, Rahab, Deborah, Ruth, Hannah, Esther, The Virtuous Woman, Mary and Martha, Mary the Mother of Jesus, The Bride of Christ.
ISBN 0-89957-302-9   224 pages

Life Principles from the Women of the Bible (Book Two)

Characters include Hagar, Lot's Wife, Rebekah, Leah, Rachel, Abigail, Bathsheba, Jezebel, Elizabeth, The Woman at the Well, Women of the Gospels, The Submisssive Wife.
ISBN 0-89957-308-8   224 pages

Other Following God™ books are available, including Leaders Guides!
Call for more information (800) 266-4977 or (423) 894-6060.
Log on to **followingGod.com** for more information about these books.